I Found It
My Pearl of Great Price

BY LIONEL JEAN-JACQUES

TEACH Services, Inc.
P U B L I S H I N G
www.TEACHServices.com • (800) 367-1844

World rights reserved. This book or any portion thereof may not be copied or reproduced in any form or manner whatever, except as provided by law, without the written permission of the publisher, except by a reviewer who may quote brief passages in a review.

The author assumes full responsibility for the accuracy of all facts and quotations as cited in this book. The opinions expressed in this book are the author's personal views and interpretations and do not necessarily reflect those of the publisher.

This book is provided with the understanding that the publisher is not engaged in giving spiritual, legal, medical, or other professional advice. If authoritative advice is needed, the reader should seek the counsel of a competent professional.

Copyright © 2023 Lionel Jean-Jacques
Copyright © 2023 TEACH Services, Inc.
ISBN-13: 978-1-4796-1565-0 (Paperback)
ISBN-13: 978-1-4796-1566-7 (ePub)
Library of Congress Control Number: 2023900993

Scripture taken from the New King James Version®. Copyright © 1982 by Thomas Nelson. Used by permission. All rights reserved.

Scripture taken from the King James Version.

The Living Bible copyright © 1971 by Tyndale House Foundation. Used by permission of Tyndale House Publishers Inc., Carol Stream, Illinois 60188. All rights reserved. The Living Bible, TLB, and The Living Bible logo are registered trademarks of Tyndale House Publishers.

Scripture quotations from New Revised Standard Version Bible, copyright © 1989 National Council of the Churches of Christ in the United States of America. Used by permission. All rights reserved worldwide.

Scripture quotations marked MSG are taken from THE MESSAGE, copyright © 1993, 2002, 2018 by Eugene H. Peterson. Used by permission of NavPress. All rights reserved. Represented by Tyndale House Publishers, Inc.

Contemporary English Version®
Copyright © 1995 American Bible Society. All rights reserved.

The ESV® Bible (The Holy Bible, English Standard Version®). ESV® Text Edition: 2016. Copyright © 2001 by Crossway, a publishing ministry of Good News Publishers. The ESV® text has been reproduced in cooperation with and by permission of Good News Publishers. Unauthorized reproduction of this publication is prohibited. All rights reserved.

Scripture quotations marked NLT are taken from the Holy Bible, New Living Translation, copyright © 1996, 2004, 2015 by Tyndale House Foundation. Used by permission of Tyndale House Publishers, Inc., Carol Stream, Illinois 60188. All rights reserved.

TEACH Services, Inc.
P U B L I S H I N G
www.TEACHServices.com • (800) 367-1844

DEDICATION

To my Dad, Aluma Jean-Jacques, and two sisters, Denise "Loulouna" Lubin and Gladys "Gros" Cesar, for your mentoring and love.

ACKNOWLEDGMENT

I want to start by thanking my awesome wife, Lynn, for your patience and enduring the suffering of loneliness while I locked myself in a room to write this manuscript. Thank you so very much, dear.

I must also thank Cathy and Joe Farkas. You two were fabulous editors and counselors. Without your generous time, patience, and suggestions, this manuscript would have taken me another ten years to write, if it ever got done at all. Again, thank you from the bottom of my heart. May God continue to bless your generous assistance to me.

TABLE OF CONTENTS

	Introduction	7
1	"Tek-Hey-Lizzie-Boy"	9
2	The Dumb Rebels	15
3	The Pearl of Great Price	19
4	The Nicodemus Syndrome	25
5	The Misunderstood God	33
6	Reasoning with God Prematurely	37
7	What Is Sin?	39
8	Shopping for Discounts	45
9	Let the Carpenter Build His Temple	49
10	Mistaken Zeal	53
11	Pseudo Judges	59
12	The Hen and the Pig	63
13	Good and Bad Religious Practices	67
14	The First and Second Deaths	73
15	What Does the Bible Mean by "Soul" and "Forever"?	83
16	Living in the Shadow of the Judgment Hour: The Story of Sodom and Gomorrah	89
17	The Wine of Babylon	93
18	The Last Message from God	99

19	No Need to Fear	109
20	God's Promises Delayed	115
Epilogue		119

INTRODUCTION

You are holding in your hand a book that is not written by a biblical scholar but by an ordinary person. In short, this book is written for simple folks just like me. I do not have biblical degrees or achievements after my name. I am simply a Bible student who has found answers to many of my questions of faith. As I studied the Word of God, I gracefully found "the Pearl of a great price."

Like me, perhaps you, too, are an ordinary person who struggles daily with life's challenges and your faith. I trust and pray this book will help you as well. I want to tell you God is in control and you should trust Him. He will reveal Himself to you personally in a way you never thought possible—if you are willing. As you study God's Word, you will be blessed much more than you ever thought possible.

You may have loved ones who are also challenged with life's difficult problems. They may have difficulties with their faith as they try to live in this uncertain world. This book is also aimed toward helping them and all those you know who are willing to search and find a better way to know the Living God for themselves.

Furthermore, this book is also written for those who once knew the Lord and seemed to have given up the faith after some struggle. Perhaps, it was simply the cares of this world that have infiltrated your life and caused you to give up altogether. These struggles may have prompted you to conclude to yourself, 'Religion does not work.'

I am in complete agreement with you. I have also come to the same conclusion. While religions do not work, I have found that following God does work. The reality is that living the life of faith has been hijacked by those who put more emphasis on the semblance of holiness, gorgeous ceremonies, and

> **The reality is that living the life of faith has been hijacked by those who put more emphasis on the semblance of holiness, gorgeous ceremonies, and outward pieties. These do not impress God or those who are searching for a real, meaningful relationship with Him.**

outward pieties. These do not impress God or those who are searching for a real, meaningful relationship with Him.

Dear reader, perhaps you are holding this book, not by accident, but because the Lord has something between its pages that can help you discover "the only true God, and Jesus Christ whom [He] has sent" (John 17:3, NKJV). In studying the Scriptures, I have discovered the Lord is a loving, merciful, and powerful Savior who is anxious to receive us with open hands.

Dear reader, in this book, I have put together a few practical lessons I have discovered from the Bible, not only to share with my family and friends, but with you as well. There is so much I do not know or understand, but what I understand, I want to share with you. I believe it is the Holy Spirit who has taught me these lessons. I hope they will strengthen your faith in God as they have done for me. This book is not extensive or exhaustive, but I pray and trust that these simple messages will help you as they have done for me.

Again, everything I have written in the book is just a brief summary of what I have learned in my Bible study from a layman's point of view. My hope is to share some of my discoveries in studying the Scripture. It is simply a preliminary resource to encourage you to study the Bible for yourself to find *your* Pearl of great price. I also hope and pray that the Spirit will put you on the right trajectory to enable you to learn these truths more deeply and bring you closer to Him. Jesus says, "I am the way, the truth, and the life. No one comes to the Father except through Me" (John 14:6, NKJV). May you find Him to be *your* way, *your* truth, and *your* life as well—for eternity. Blessings!

CHAPTER 1

"TEK-HEY-LIZZIE-BOY"

When I was growing up, I never thought about religion. Like the sneaker company Nike, I would "just do it"—I did whatever I was told to do. Going to church was just a way of life for me. My only goal was to immigrate to the United States of America someday. My father had immigrated to New York City in the mid-1960s. My dream finally came true on April 29, 1969. I could hardly believe I was going to America!

I can still vividly remember how bright the cabin of that huge Trans Caribbean Airways airplane was—at least from my perspective. In the little town where I grew up, there were constant blackouts and therefore the need to use candles. I have come to understand the blackouts I experienced in my early life were more than physical; they were mental and spiritual as well. It would take me many years to begin to understand how blind I was in many areas of my life, especially spiritually. Even though I grew up in a religious home and culture and attended a Catholic parochial school, Bible reading was anathema to us.

During that period of my life, I didn't know a word of English—well, except "Tek-hey-lizzie-boy." I must have heard that phrase or one that sounded like it from a neighbor who "spoke English" or one of the tourists somewhere along the way. Notwithstanding, I loved to show off in front of friends and display my prowess and proficiency in the English language, so I repeated my newly found sophisticated "English" phrase over and over again.

It took me years, perhaps decades, to 1) know how to spell my prized phrase, 2) find out what it meant, and 3) most importantly, how to pronounce it correctly. Please do not get too far ahead of me. Yes, the phrase was "Take it easy boy." I still feel a bit foolish thinking how wrong I had been with my "Tek-hey-lizzie-boy" lingo. Nevertheless, I didn't have a clue that I was making a fool of myself every time I blurted out what I thought was an intelligent English phrase (please continue to read after you finish laughing).

Even though I attended a parochial school in the country of my birth, I was never once taught the wonderful lessons from the Bible. I was taught a lot of traditions of the church from its Catechism, but not the Bible. Like many others, in all types of religion, I was taught a lot of religious ceremonies and human traditions. Again, like many others, I just accepted these dogmas from my religious teachers as if they were the oracles of God. However, my deep longings and questions were never answered. I was never satisfied with the answers of humanity. Whatever was taught seemed like a bunch of never-ending puzzles without an end.

In retrospect, I have found that most of those religious traditions can have a powerful, negative impact on the life of a person for a long time. It was like a trap that kept me from ever being able to escape. That's one of the reasons I encourage everyone to diligently study the Word of God, the Bible, for yourself to be set free from human dogmas and inventions. Otherwise, we will be kept in the dark about what God has done, is doing, and will do for every one of His children.

That is the reason, during my formative years, I had no idea how earnestly God searches for every one of His created beings. It took years for me to recognize how the Lord was shepherding me and everyone else He created. Furthermore, today, I recognize His loving, patient, merciful hands toward not only those who accept Him as their Savior but even those who do not know Him yet or have rejected Him altogether.

Growing up, I always had tons of questions about God. It never occurred to me that His Word had the answers to my soul's longing. That is why I am so glad to write this small book to share with you how the Lord has answered my questions from the Bible. At least there are sufficient answers in the Bible to show us the way to heaven. I am sure new and more perplexing questions may arise, but I have confidence that God will answer them, too, as He has done in the past. Thank God, He has given me the assurance of salvation, and if some of the other questions that may arise are not answered immediately in this life, He will answer them in the world to come.

One of the first lessons I learned when I began studying the Bible is that God wants to save everyone. "For God so loved the world, that he gave his only begotten Son, that whosoever believeth in him should not perish, but have everlasting life. For God sent not his Son into the world to condemn the world; but that the world through him might be saved" (John 3:16, 17, KJV).

The apostle Paul chimed in: "For by grace are ye saved through faith; and that not of yourselves: *it is* the gift of God: Not of works, lest any man should boast. For we are his workmanship, created in Christ Jesus unto good works, which God hath before ordained that we should walk in them" (Eph. 2:8–10). The Bible says God saves us willingly and freely, without any obligation on our part when we respond to His drawing us to Him.

I further discovered God is able "to keep you from falling, and to present you faultless before the presence of His glory with exceeding joy" (Jude 24). He has invested His greatest heavenly assets to save sinners like us. God laid on the line His love and reputation when He offered His one and only Divine Son to save us from the ruin of sin. And He is more willing to accomplish His salvation for all who are willing to be saved—yes, "saved," "taken to heaven," or whatever traditional vernacular you prefer to use. In my humble opinion, these truths should be the first things a new person in Christ who is seeking to know God pursues before getting into other complicated subject matter.

In my trek to understand the Bible, I learned it is like a language. It has its own grammar and lexicon (the totality of words in a given language, with accompanying rules). The Bible uses its own linguistic tools, such as parables, allegories, imageries, and poetries, just to name a few. It is not a good practice to bring one's own lexicon or linguistic rules to interpret the Bible, especially if one does not have a Hebrew, Aramaic, or Greek background. In studying, one must allow the Bible to interpret itself.

I learned the Bible is inspired by the Holy Spirit (see 2 Tim. 3:16, 17; 2 Peter 1:20, 21), and we are not to come to the study with our own private interpretations. Since "spiritual things are spiritually discerned" (1 Cor. 2:14), we must become born again by the Holy Spirit before we can fully understand the Bible's messages. We also need to be willing to accept the will of God before we can truly advance in our knowledge of His Word. Some were questioning Jesus' authority, and He said, "If anyone wills to do His will, he shall know concerning the doctrine, whether it is from God or *whether* I speak on My own *authority*" (John 7:17, NKJV).

Furthermore, I learned I am a sinner saved by grace. I know I am not fully where I ought to be as a follower of God, but praise Him, for I am not where I used to be. God is still working with me. Praise His holy name! Our heavenly Father and loving Savior, Jesus Christ, are constantly seeking to get our attention and teach and lead us on an ever upward path to eternal life. God also leads us through our most difficult journeys in life and promises to be with us until the end.

The Lord not only taught me in His Word to set me free from my spiritual darkness, but He also healed me physically. Before I move on to more of my biblical discoveries, let me share a brief story about how the Lord helped me with a physical illness. We read in the Bible about how Christ performed miracles in His day. He healed those who were afflicted. We may wonder at times, 'Why doesn't Jesus perform these same miracles today?' I believe He still does, but perhaps by different means.

    I would like to share my experience of how Jesus Christ performed a miracle for me recently. For most of my life, I have been relatively healthy. However, as I turned 62 years old, my health suddenly took a downturn I had never experienced before.

    First, my vision began to get blurry. I was unable to drive safely, especially at night and during rain. I went to several eye doctors for examinations. They simply gave me new prescriptions for a new pair of glasses. I had no success with these new glasses. I fainted twice during that time period. I began to feel very weak. My blood pressure skyrocketed. A friend who was concerned about me suggested I see an ophthalmologist. She spent a long time examining my eyes, trying to figure out why I was unable to see clearly. Finally, after having spent an extended amount of time with me, she recommended I get an MRI.

    The MRI revealed that my pituitary gland was inflamed. The pituitary gland is a small, bean-shaped gland situated at the base of a brain, somewhere behind the nose and between the ears. Accordingly, this small gland influences nearly every part of the body. The hormones it produces help regulate important functions, such as growth and blood pressure. Mine had grown so large that it was pushing up my optic nerve, interfering with my sight.

    When I finally went to a neurosurgeon, he told me I "may" need surgery. Instead of doing the surgery right away, he prescribed a drug that was supposed to shrink the tumor. After three months, with my vision deteriorating, I turned to a nurse friend who recommended I see another neurosurgeon who would be able to help. There was another obstacle. It turned out this new neurosurgeon did not accept my insurance. I felt I had hit another roadblock. Nevertheless, I trusted the Lord anyway.

    The doctor told me to come and see him despite the insurance issue. He did a thorough examination of the problem, free of charge. He also recommended I see another neurosurgeon who deals with these cases "all the time." Again, it turned out this doctor was also not in my insurance network. Despite that, he committed to help me. He said the tumor needed to be removed immediately, or else I could lose my sight permanently. Of course, I was very concerned when I received this news.

However, I was encouraged by many people who began to pray earnestly for me. Finally, after contacting my insurance company, the doctor called me to give me the good news. My insurance company had granted him approval to do the surgery. That's when I recognized, more vividly, the Lord was with me and blessing me all along. As one can imagine, I could not stop praising the Lord for His leading and blessings. However, the Lord was not yet finished blessing me.

The neurosurgeon needed an ENT (ear, nose, and throat) physician to assist him in the operation. He assured me he would find one of the best ENTs around. A few weeks later, he called to give me the good news. Not only had he found an excellent ENT; he also had scheduled the surgery. Praise the Lord!

The day after the surgery, I was able to see so clearly. I could not stop talking about it or praising the Lord. A couple people commented that even my voice sounded stronger than before. I think it was because I could not stop telling people what a great miracle the Lord had done for me!

Dear reader, I thank God for the opportunity to share with you what He has done for me physically. Physical cures are important yet temporal. I put more value on what He has taught me from His inspired Word. When He cures us spiritually, that will be for eternity. I want to share these precious eternal promises with you as well. Now, let's get started.

"Now to Him who is able to keep you from stumbling, and to present you faultless before the presence of His glory with exceeding joy, To God our Savior, Who alone is wise, be glory and majesty, dominion and power, both now and forever. Amen" (Jude 24, 25, NKJV). I like the first word of that passage, "Now," don't you? We do not have to wait for long. God is able and willing to redeem and save us today; more specifically, now—this moment. Here is a simple prayer you can pray just now: "Dear Lord Jesus, I know I am a sinner and ask for Your forgiveness. I believe You died for my sins and rose from the dead. I turn from my sins and invite You to come into my heart and life. I want to trust and follow You as my Lord and Savior. Amen."

> Dear reader, I thank God for the opportunity to share with you what He has done for me physically. Physical cures are important yet temporal. I put more value on what He has taught me from His inspired Word. When He cures us spiritually, that will be for eternity.

Please also notice the last word of this passage in Jude: "Amen." The Semitic root of the word "amen" is derived from a word meaning "firm," "fixed," or "sure." The Hebrew verb also means "to be reliable" and "to be trusted." The

Greek Old Testament usually translated "amen" as "so be it." In the English Bible, it has often been rendered as "verily" or "truly."

In other words, the One who graciously declared this promise is reliable and trustworthy. His promises are firm, fixed, and sure. God has not refused or lost an honest soul who put his o her trust in Him. You can build your faith on His promises. Now, do you see what a little study or research can yield from God's Word, the Bible? Amen. So be it!

When I hear someone make an "interesting" statement about the Bible, it reminds me of my "Tek-hey-lizzie-boy" days. Beloved, we are to beware, lest we think we know the Bible when we are actually making fools of ourselves, at least in the sight of God and the heavenly angels.

Furthermore, we are to be careful about what we think we heard and believe before going around repeating it. Many times, we think we have the living truth and go around preaching it to others as the gospel of Jesus Christ. Sometime later, to our regret, we discover we have been disseminating foolishness, or worse, spurious doctrines to other people.

Let me quickly add that in God, there is hope for us. The Holy Spirit can elevate the most simple-minded person who puts his or her trust in Him. Praise the Lord! I am deeply convinced and confident that if God can take an ignorant, backward young man like me and teach him the way to eternal life, He can do the same for you and anyone else as well.

CHAPTER 2

THE DUMB REBELS

The literal meaning of "dumb" is "unable to speak." When the word "dumb" is used as slang or an adjective, it has an altogether different meaning. For example, when a student says, "I'm too dumb to pass the test," it means "stupid" or "unintelligent."

It is not uncommon for a good parent or teacher to instruct children not to ever call themselves or anyone else dumb or stupid. After all, God did not make anyone dumb or stupid. "God did not make junk."

Proverbs generally uses the more gentle word "simple" to convey this idea. Perhaps Solomon meant that such a person is not generally dumb or stupid but has a lack of information or instruction. I suppose it is in this context that I use the word "dumb." I hope.

However, I must confess, the more I study the Bible, the more I personally find, while God did not create us dumb or stupid, many of us, including myself, have made a lot of stupid decisions throughout our lives. As Solomon, "the wisest man," put it, "Lo, this only have I found, that God hath made man upright; but they have sought out many inventions" (Eccles. 7:29). As the Living Bible (TLB) puts it, "I found that though God has made men upright, each has turned away to follow his own downward road." As a result of this "downward" direction, we have become very stupid—I mean simple. I am not just referring to hardcore evil people or atheists, but followers of God as well.

Take the prophet Jonah, for example. God called this man to go and preach to the city of Nineveh. In all honesty, humanly speaking, Jonah felt Nineveh was unworthy of any warning or favor of God. In fact, God himself described Nineveh as a city of wickedness. Besides, Nineveh did not treat Jonah's people, Israel, very well. In actuality, Jonah simply hated these foreigners. Nevertheless, when God commands us to do something, we should not try to evaluate or revert back to our own biases or judgment to decide whether to obey Him or not. Indeed, instead of obeying God's commands, Jonah tried to flee elsewhere from Him.

Let me quote the passage just to remind you of Jonah's foolishness:

> Now the word of the LORD came to Jonah the son of Amittai, saying, "Arise, go to Nineveh, that great city, and cry out against it; for their wickedness has come up before Me." But Jonah arose to flee to Tarshish from the presence of the LORD. He went down to Joppa, and found a ship going to Tarshish; so he paid the fare, and went down into it, to go with them to Tarshish from the presence of the LORD. (Jonah 1:1–3, NKJV)

Did you get the import of these words? Jonah tried to flee and hide from the omniscient (all-knowing) God.

At this point, I need to tread very carefully, lest I judge Jonah too harshly and reveal my own hypocrisy. Nevertheless, I must clearly write it, for I do not know any other way to put it: *Rebellion makes a person stupid.* I mean, what other word can be used for a man who thinks he can flee and hide from a God who is not just omnipotent (all-powerful) but omniscient as well? Only the Lord knows how many times I have personally found myself rationalizing His clear. unambiguous commandments to pursue my own rebellious ways. Had it not been for a merciful God who deals constantly with me as He did with Jonah, I don't know where I would have ended up today.

I write these words to you, reader, praying and hoping you, too, can see and experience the goodness and mercifulness of our loving God. "If You, Lord, should mark iniquities, O Lord, who could stand? But there is forgiveness with You, That You may be feared" (Ps. 130:3, 4). One has to be "simple" or drinking the wine of Babylon to reject such a loving and merciful God.

I further write this book to share with all who find themselves reading these pages about how God is merciful toward me and any others who are willing to follow Him. Not only will He forgive our past foolishness and rebellion, but He will guide us into assimilating His fabulous, righteous character as revealed in the Bible. If we are willing, God will remove our rebellious, stubborn heart and give us a heart of righteousness.

Furthermore, God will show us that we don't see people as He sees them (of course, we need to let Him correct that). The story of Jonah ended very well for the city of Nineveh. Read the book; it is only four short chapters. I do not want to spoil this wonderful lesson, though I can only hope it also ended well for Jonah—and everyone else who has found themselves in a similar situation to that of the runaway prophet.

CHAPTER 3

THE PEARL OF GREAT PRICE

The kingdom of heaven surpasses every other prize one can imagine obtaining. Jesus told a parable about a merchantman seeking goodly pearls. "The kingdom of heaven is like unto a merchant man, seeking goodly pearls: Who, when he had found one pearl of great price, went and sold all that he had, and bought it" (Matt. 13:45, 46, KJV). This parable illustrates the great value of the kingdom of God. Jesus Christ Himself is the Pearl of great price. When we find Jesus and accept Him as our Savior and Lord, we have found priceless treasure.

I found my Pearl of great price in Oceanside, California. I was serving in the US Marine Corps when the phone rang. The voice on the other end invited me to a Bible seminar. I was skeptical at first, but I knew the Lord had put in my heart the desire to know Him better. The seminar offered me an opportunity to study the Bible in a more systematic way.

It did not take long for me to get enthralled with what the Bible had to teach on important topics, such as why we were created, salvation, what happens when we die, and heaven and hell, just to name a few. I also learned Jesus was in heaven preparing a place for His followers and is coming back again to take us to be with Him there. I thank God for giving "understanding to the simple" (Ps. 119:130). My Bible studies offered up so many answers to my many unanswered questions I had held in my heart. That is why I want to share. I cannot and dare not keep all these "gems" to myself.

I finally learned how to dig for what the Bible called "the pearl of great price." And I found that the Pearl was Jesus, whom I was seeking all this time. I further learned that the most important lesson in life is to find salvation in Him. When we find and accept Him, He gives us eternal life by His grace, "without money and without price" (Isa. 55:1).

I also found that God was the One who was seeking me. It impressed me that my salvation does not depend on my own efforts or good works but on His desire and power to save. No matter what our clerics have taught us now or in the past, it is God alone who takes the initiative in searching for us and saves us by His grace.

Another foundational lesson I learned was, just like a child, no one is born already capable of reading. Before a child, or an adult, for that matter, can read, he or she must learn how to do it from someone else. And incidentally, that applies not just to learning how to read but anything else that is necessary to know in this life. Furthermore, we all need teachers. The best teachers use appropriate tools to educate their pupils. Otherwise, we will reach various interpretations and meanings that may or may not answer our inquiries. It is essential to ask and receive the best answers to the most important questions of life, such as, Why are we here? What does the future hold for us? Or, How can we have eternal life?

This is what will happen when we respond to the Lord pursuing us. He will teach us the way to eternal life. The Lord Jesus Christ, through the Holy Spirit, answered my most intimate, prayerful questions about the meaning of my existence on this earth. Our wonderful, beneficent Teacher can teach you about the meaning of your existence as well. I understand some people purport to have "taught themselves" how to read and do many other things without God. The truth of the matter is if people like this have truly learned anything about why they are here, the most likely explanation is our unseen Creator and Teacher has taught them without them even acknowledging Him, let alone giving Him the credit. That is the reason the Bible indicates our Father in heaven "makes His sun to rise on the evil and on the good and sends rain on the just and on the unjust" (Matt. 5:45).

Incidentally, life makes no sense if there is not an intelligent being who created us and started all of what we know and see in existence. It's absolute lunacy to speak about a beginning that started in a chaotic, disorganized way. I understand many believe in this kind of beginning. Is it any wonder, then, that our society is so lacking in moral absolutes? Indeed, that explains why the whole world is in such a moral quandary! I have found that the

> **Incidentally, life makes no sense if there is not an intelligent being who created us and started all of what we know and see in existence. It's absolute lunacy to speak about a beginning that started in a chaotic, disorganized way. I understand many believe in this kind of beginning. Is it any wonder, then, that our society is so lacking in moral absolutes?**

Bible is the only book that has given us a real, meaningful explanation of a loving Creator who not only made us but also sustains us, whether or not we acknowledge Him. Yes, He is still in control today, even amid all the troubles we experience in this world.

Reader, I can almost hear you ask, just as I did, "If God is so loving why is there so much evil in the world?" This question, too, my heavenly Father has answered in His Word. We must be willing to search diligently and earnestly to find God's answer, just as we would if we were searching for gold or pearls. The Bible charges us to be diligent students. This means before we can learn these important lessons, we must be *willing* to learn.

The Creator gave us a most wonderful, powerful gift: the power of choice. God will not trample on our free will. It is our decision to exercise it, for better or worse. Many love to assert the fact that "this is a free country." They can do whatever they wish. Don't you find it interesting how we vehemently protest when we think someone or some government entity is trampling upon our free choice? I have heard and continue to hear the indignation from many, including faithful Christians, when that occurs.

Yet, we get equally annoyed, to put it mildly, when someone suggests we try to live our lives God's way. He's the One who gave us the gift of free choice in the first place. Then we turn around and blame Him for all the choices we and other people make to bring many of these troubles upon ourselves. We cherish our power of choice to do whatever we want to do and when we want to do it. And we say, "No one has the right to tell us what to do." We should consider and admit that perhaps God's way is the best.

Indeed, God had given us this great power, but with power comes great responsibility. If not exercised prudently, it can bring enormous disaster, as we see so often today. Let me add just a little more.

I once heard a great scholar and teacher put it this way: God had three possible choices or options. First, God could have chosen not to create any intelligent beings and live in the universe alone; He did not choose that option. Second, God could have created beings like robots and program them to love and obey Him on command; He did not choose that option either. The third option was a huge risk, but in His wisdom, God chose to create intelligent beings in His image and likeness, with the power of choice.

These beings chose to exercise their God-given choice. Yes, true choice sometimes has consequences and unfavorable possibilities. Otherwise, it's not authentically free. The consequences are evident for all to see and experience in this world. Let me hasten to say God does have a plan to eradicate sin without trampling on our will to choose. He will not end this world prematurely without making sure all have freely made the choice for or against His government. The experiment must run its course until everyone exercises their choice to either follow God or completely rebel against His laws and ways.

God promised that sin will be eradicated at its proper time. One may ask, "Why does God allow this tragedy to go on for so long?" The Bible gives this comprehensive answer:

> The Lord is not slack concerning his promise, as some men count slackness; but is longsuffering to us-ward, not willing that any should perish, but that all should come to repentance. But the day of the Lord will come as a thief in the night; in the which the heavens shall pass away with a great noise, and the elements shall melt with fervent heat, the earth also and the works that are therein shall be burned up. Seeing then that all these things shall be dissolved, what manner of persons ought ye to be in all holy conversation and godliness. (2 Peter 3:9–11)

We have the capacity to hasten that day by making our choice without delay. I learned Bible study helps us to know how to make intelligent choices concerning this most important subject. The Bible gives eternal wisdom to understand many of these difficult subjects. "Study to show thyself approved unto God, a workman that needeth not to be ashamed, rightly dividing the word of truth" (2 Tim. 2:15, KJV). This text suggests there is a right way to "divide" or interpret the teachings of the Bible.

Naturally, that would indicate one can choose to "wrongly divide" the word of truth. Otherwise, those who choose to reject the Bible would not have come up with so many diverse, dangerous, speculative answers. Is there any wonder we have so many spurious doctrines and errors in the religious and secular realms about the Bible today? I maintain that only the Holy Spirit can reveal the Bible's true meaning to the sincere seeker. Paul characterized it this way:

> Now we have received, not the spirit of the world, but the Spirit who is from God, that we might know the things that have been freely given to us by God. These things we also speak, not in words which man's wisdom teaches but which the Holy Spirit teaches, comparing spiritual things with spiritual. But the natural man does not receive the things of the Spirit of God, for they are foolishness to him; nor can he know *them*, because they are spiritually discerned. (1 Cor. 2:12–14, NKJV)

In giving us *the* most important learning tool, the Bible, the Holy Spirit employed approximately three dozen different authors who wrote over a period of 1,600 years. "Knowing this first, that no prophecy of the scripture is of any private interpretation. For the prophecy came not in old time by the will of man: but holy men of God spoke as they were moved by the Holy Ghost" (1 Peter 1:20, 21, KJV). Since the Holy Spirit was the one who inspired all these holy people to write the Bible, it is logical, therefore, to have Him help us interpret and understand the Scriptures.

Yes, let me emphasize this again. This wonderful book, inspired by the Holy Spirit, is given to teach us everything we need to know about the meaning of our existence on this planet and much, much more. There is a right and wrong way to interpret the Scriptures. Without the Holy Spirit teaching us, we will come up with all kinds of obscure opinions and traditions.

The good news is the Lord does not leave us alone to grapple in the darkness of error. God's love and grace pursue us from the beginning until the end of our lives. Again, we need to choose and make some effort to know the truth of the Bible, but it is God who initiates the effort. This truth is not only found in the New Testament. "I will seek that which was lost, and bring again that which was driven away, and will bind up that which was broken, and will strengthen that which was sick" (Ezek. 34:16). If we do not resist, the Holy Spirit is given to us to lead us into the kingdom of God. This affirmation gets better: "For the Son of man is come to seek and to save that which was lost" (Luke 19:10).

When we choose to acknowledge our beneficent Creator, who initiated this search for His lost sheep, then He begins the process of revealing Himself to us more fully through the Son. God accomplishes this process by changing the hearts (minds) and perspectives of those who choose to see instead of remaining blind. "And Jesus said, 'For judgment I am come into this world, that they which see not might see; and that they which see might be made blind" (John 9:39). As stated before, this process is called "being born again." That brings us to the next chapter of this book.

CHAPTER 4

THE NICODEMUS SYNDROME

The account of Nicodemus' discussion with Jesus is found in John 3. Regarding the title of this chapter, surely you have experienced or heard someone affected by a fever or flu. Some viruses such as the bubonic plague, HIV, or AIDS—and we cannot forget COVID-19—are extremely dangerous. I would like to propose that "Nicodemus Syndrome" is even more hazardous than those are. While the other viruses can hurt us physically, Nicodemus Syndrome can hurt us not only physically but spiritually as well.

The gospel of John records this story about a man named Nicodemus. He was a Pharisee. You could not find a more religious bunch of people in those days. Nicodemus held an exceedingly prominent position in the Jewish nation. He was educated and an honored member of the national council. Though he was rich, learned, and honored, he had been stirred by the teaching of Jesus. Apparently, these teachings greatly impressed him, and he was determined to learn more of these wonderful truths, so He visited Jesus at night.

Nicodemus came to Jesus at night because he did not want his colleagues to find out he had visited the Savior. This ultra-conservative religious man knew he was missing something. His heart yearned for something that eluded him. Unbeknown to him, it was the heavenly Father who drew him to the Messiah. Please remember it is always God who draws people to Himself. "There is none who understands; There is none who seeks after God" (Rom. 3:11).

Nicodemus started his conversation with Jesus with a philosophical note, hoping to impress Him: "Rabbi, we know that You are a teacher come from God; for no one can do these signs that You do unless God is with him" (John 3:2). Please notice Nicodemus only recognized Jesus as a rabbi (teacher), not as the Messiah—the Savior of the world.

Jesus replied, "Most assuredly, I say to you, unless one is born again, he cannot see the kingdom of God" (verse 3). He advanced an unwelcome concept that required a shocking change in perspective. It was not something simple or easy for Nicodemus or those who suffer from this syndrome to grasp and accept right away. He asked Jesus, "How can a man be born when he is old? Can he enter a second time into his mother's womb and be born?" (verse 4).

Jesus' reply to the incredulous Pharisee was direct and decisive:

> Most assuredly, I say to you, unless one is born of water and the Spirit, he cannot enter the kingdom of God. That which is born of the flesh is flesh, and that which is born of the Spirit is spirit. Do not marvel that I said to you, "You must be born again." The wind blows where it wishes, and you hear the sound of it, but cannot tell where it comes from and where it goes. So is everyone who is born of the Spirit. (John 3:5–8, NKJV)

The statement "You must be born of water and the Spirit" leaves no room to wiggle out of making that critical decision to get baptized. The meaning is clear. A true child of God must be baptized by water and filled by the Holy Spirit. There are no ifs, ands, or buts about it. The only exception would be, of course, if you are like the thief on the cross, who did not have a chance to come down to receive water baptism. That thief certainly experienced the Holy Spirit's baptism. The options are we will either be born again or perish. It is worth knowing right from the start that being born again is not the destination of knowing God; it is simply the beginning of the journey. While this new birth is the beginning of our journey, when switching to God's side, He has so much more to teach and give us.

Like most of us, Nicodemus had been satisfied with cold, lifeless, religious ceremonies that conceal true worship of God. He did not know this until the interview with Christ. To be born again, we must first recognize our condition as sinners and violators of God's revealed will. A fundamental human problem is our unwillingness to acknowledge there is something seriously wrong with us. We are in desperate need of forgiveness and reconciliation with our Creator. I have learned that even forgiven sinners must constantly recognize we need to experience God's mercies and grace daily (see Luke 9:23; 1 Cor. 15:31).

In other words, we need to be stripped of our semblance of holiness and be converted through God's righteousness. It takes a change from our ways of following the maxims of this world to accepting God's perspective by serving Him, our Lord and Savior, Jesus Christ. Another way to say this is we need to switch from following the world, which is the evil kingdom of Satan, to following the righteous kingdom of God. Many people came to God trying to impress Him with their piety and religious devotion. Like many who come to God, Nicodemus came with his own "fig leaf" covering. Here lies the first symptom of Nicodemus Syndrome: We think we are good enough to atone for our sins and go to heaven.

Nicodemus Syndrome affects not only the unreligious but also those who have grown up with deep religious ideals and convictions. If we are not careful, this confidence can cause us to become arrogant and proud of our religious and national heritage, making us feel we have no need for reformation. Moreover, we can become callous and resistant to accepting new ideas, thinking we are good enough and need nothing. Some of us like to compare ourselves with those whom we think are worse sinners than we are. We compare ourselves with ourselves. While we may feel this is right, the Bible warns us this is not wise (see 2 Cor. 10:12).

To be safe, we need to compare ourselves with our only pattern, Jesus Christ. We are to keep our eyes on Him to be changed into His image (see 2 Cor. 3:18). Like many others, when cutting truth is brought home to the conscience, it is revealed that natural humanity doesn't receive the things of the Spirit of God. A person does not feel the need to understand or respond to spiritual things. The real reason for this kind of attitude is "the natural man does not receive the things of the Spirit of God, for they are foolishness to him; nor can he know *them*, because they are spiritually discerned" (1 Cor. 2:14).

The moment we make the decision to accept and follow God, He begins to change us into the image of His dear Son, Jesus Christ. That is what the word "conversion" means. However, throughout the journey, we must cooperate with Him. This needs to be a daily experience. We cannot believe in God only one day a week in church. Many have started this solemn journey only to take their eyes from the Captain of their salvation and end up losing their way.

We can compare this phenomenon with a big ship leaving a port to travel on a long journey. On the way to its destination, the wind and waves imperceptibly move the ship from its course. The good news is our Captain, Jesus, knows the way perfectly. He knows how to use His holy gyrocompass to navigate the treacherous waters and dangerous winds of life to get us to our peaceful, long-awaited journey's end. That is the reason we need to cooperate with Captain Jesus, not only daily, but every moment of our lives.

Make no mistake about it. Nicodemus was a good man. He was searching for spiritual regeneration. Although he did not immediately surrender his life to Jesus that night, He did eventually follow the Master. It took some time before Nicodemus was cured of his syndrome, but he finally accepted Jesus and the real truth of salvation. Scripture testifies to the fact that when Jesus' disciples had forsaken Him at His crucifixion, Nicodemus was one of two prominent men in Israel who stepped forward to honor Him with a proper burial (see John 19:38–42). There is hope for us, too!

In heaven and the new earth, there will be an exceptional group of citizens who have allowed the Holy Spirit to cure them of the syndrome of self-righteousness. This cure (being born again) will not only help us resist the temptations of this world but also serve as the passport or visa to enter the kingdom of God.

Unfortunately, unlike Nicodemus, many turn away from Jesus unconverted during their entire lives while thinking they are "fine" with God. Some of those are showered with flatteries or words of praise on earth, especially during their funerals. It is common to hear at funerals words of praise paying tribute to a "great" man or woman who has died. Their eulogies are filled with accolades on how good they were when they were alive on earth. Most were "pillars in their community," we are told. Nevertheless, were they born again?

We often hear these deceased ones are transported immediately to heaven and enjoying holy bliss with God while they are looking down on us miserable living ones. In one of his parables, Jesus debunks this deceptive idea once and for all, at least for those who make their calling and election sure before that great day:

> Not everyone who says to Me, "Lord, Lord," shall enter the kingdom of heaven, but he who does the will of My Father in heaven. Many will say to Me in that day, "Lord, Lord, have we not prophesied in Your name, cast out demons in Your name, and done many wonders in Your name?" And then I will declare to them, "I never knew you; depart from Me, you who practice lawlessness!" (Matt. 7:21–23, NKJV)

Worldly-minded people operate on the premise of being "good" in their society. They believe they are good enough to go to heaven immediately after death. However, Jesus said being "so-called good" is not enough. We must do the will of God. Incidentally, what is the will of God? What does God require of us? Jesus told us, "This is the will of the Father who sent Me, that of all He has given Me I should lose nothing, but should raise it up at the last day. And this is the will of Him who sent Me, that everyone who sees the Son and believes in Him may have everlasting life; and I will raise him up at the last day" (John 6:39, 40).

Elsewhere, Jesus said, "At that day you will know that I *am* in My Father, and you in Me, and I in you. He who has My commandments and keeps them, it is he who loves Me. And he who loves Me will be loved by My Father, and I will love him and manifest Myself to him" (14:20, 21).

I know by experience that our old ways and set ideas are not easy to give up, no matter how wrong they are. Long-cherished ideas have a way of shackling us to fatal delusions. Only the truth in the Word of God, by the Holy Spirit, can penetrate and unshackle the chains that keep us in this perpetual bondage. Dear Reader, God did this for me, and He can do it for you also.

The Bible is filled with God's loving warnings against following abominable practices and dangerous, unbiblical ideas from so-called intellectual men and women. We are to beware lest we find ourselves following compromised ideas from these false prophets and so-called "great minds" of the world. The Bible categorically dismisses the idea that "I am okay, and you are okay; just try to be a good person." We are to examine our spiritual state to see if we are in the faith (see 2 Cor. 13:6). When we are not born again, arrogance creeps in. We become callous—immune from the Spirit's promptings. We develop gaps in our spiritual ideals. That is the reason we can be strict and unmovable in some darling religious tradition yet totally blind in some other important areas of our lives.

> I know by experience that our old ways and set ideas are not easy to give up, no matter how wrong they are. Long-cherished ideas have a way of shackling us to fatal delusions. Only the truth in the Word of God, by the Holy Spirit, can penetrate and unshackle the chains that keep us in this perpetual bondage.

For example, it is common to hear these religious folks extolling the virtues of the Ten Commandments. However, upon closer examination, these same people abhor many of these wonderful commandments. Their profession of faith is simply a ruse to protect reputation. This group has come to believe evil is good and good is evil as long as it benefits them. The apostle John characterized the test of knowing God this way:

> And He Himself is the propitiation for our sins, and not for ours only but also for the whole world. Now by this we know that we know Him, if we keep His commandments. He who says, "I know Him," and does not keep His commandments, is a liar, and the truth is not in him. But whoever

keeps His word, truly the love of God is perfected in him. By this we know that we are in Him. He who says he abides in Him ought himself also to walk just as He walked. (1 John 2:2–6, NKJV)

"Jesus Christ *is* the same yesterday, today, and forever" (Heb. 13:8). We are warned not to be "carried about with various and strange doctrines" (verse 9). Is this passage talking about us? Have we been carried about with strange doctrines? Do we have a different understanding of who God or Jesus is today than we had when we first believed? Have we allowed "various and strange doctrines" from purported Bible scholars or philosophers to creep into our minds—to change our saving, loving Lord into a permissive, careless deity?

False Christs and prophets have convinced many to believe in a modern, humanistic God. I am personally glad God is not a capricious being like we are. This deception can have a powerful hold on our psyches, considering our modern world with its spurious belief systems. These systems can be a powerful substance like an addiction or strong drug. We need an even more powerful substance: the power of the Holy Spirit to make radical changes in our hearts.

As we grow in grace as trusting believers, we should not change God's words to make Him or the Bible more acceptable. His message of love should not be changed. The message should change us into the image of Christ, not some bogus "god" who allows anything. God says, "For I *am* the Lord, I do not change; Therefore you are not consumed, O sons of Jacob" (Mal. 3:6). The Lord is a loving God who is not willing for His created beings to be consumed or lost. We need to embrace and reconsider who He is and who we are in Him.

In our quest to not offend others, sometimes we do not share what Jesus said to Nicodemus. Many have been "baptized" as babies. How can babies decide to accept Jesus as their Lord and Savior? We cannot replace the baptism of the Holy Spirit with sprinkling. Many who feel a lack of the Spirit are trying to compensate with a shaking, rocking, and feel-good religion. However, that good feeling will not replace our emptiness or wipe out our predicament. The apostle Paul said, "Beware lest anyone cheat you through philosophy and empty deceit" (Col. 2:8). We must constantly be on guard lest we find ourselves believing in a Jesus of our own making or worshiping a God made with human hands (see 1 Cor. 8:5, 6).

Another example is how some music is so vile, sensual, and depraved, yet the performers have no hesitation to thank "the man upstairs" when honored with an award. Reader, have you ever wondered, 'Who is that "man" upstairs?'

They act as if God was inspiring these vile lyrics that are calculated to ruin their listeners. Let us give God true honor and glory. His way is not our filthy ways.

I have learned Satan starts out small to infiltrate the unsuspected. The enemy knows no one comes to sudden ruin. It takes time to corrupt the soul. Gradually, the devil perverts even the innocent. One departure from principle begins the journey. Our love for God and that for which He stands deteriorates slowly until we slip away to the camp of the enemy. Corruption and dishonest communication become normal. We know habits develop slowly. They progress by practice and repetition. Habits become character, and character becomes destiny.

Finally, we need to remember eternity is a long time. And because of eternity, we need to reconsider our priorities. We need to have the right attitude; we need to make up our minds this side of eternity whether we will abide by God's conditions. The truth changes not. We should not try to change it. Jesus does not change. He is still the same always.

Beloved, this is worth repeating: God does not change to accommodate evildoings. He is "the same yesterday, today, and forever" (Heb. 13:8). Today is the day of conversion and salvation. Paul succinctly counseled us, "Today, if you will hear His voice, Do not harden your hearts" (3:15). May the Lord help us to have receptive hearts.

CHAPTER 5

THE MISUNDERSTOOD GOD

One of the most pervasive teachings in the minds of many is that the God of the Old Testament is a very stern, cruel being. In contrast, the God of the New Testament is a loving, forgiving Savior. Popular myths are accepted instead of God's Word. After I started studying the Bible, I quickly saw the God of the Old Testament is the same loving, merciful God of the New Testament. Friends, when we live with our false assumptions long enough, we become deceived. When we live with errors long enough, we begin to believe them—sincerely believe them! We can't even see help is near.

Why did I misunderstand God? I would like to suggest to you three reasons why we often misunderstand God:

First, we misunderstand God because the sins in our lives deaden or deafen our perceptions of Him and make it difficult to hear His voice.

Second, not only do our own personal sins blind us regarding hope and faith, but living in a sinful environment also affects our perceptions. You see, our long-term entrenchment in a sinful situation makes us misunderstand God. At times, we even "humanize" God with our own faulty characteristics.

Not only do the sins in our lives and those surrounding us cause us to misunderstand God, but third, we confuse God's voice with the voice of the enemy, Satan. We think of God's favor as His disapproval. We confuse light for darkness. Consequently, we listen to the enemy when he is whispering evil intentions about our merciful Benefactor.

We are even told by some religious leaders that it does not matter what we believe anymore. Truth is so watered down, we cannot even discern it!

> We are even told by some religious leaders that it does not matter what we believe anymore. Truth is so watered down, we cannot even discern it!

It is true that we find many examples of Jesus healing and forgiving people in the New Testament. There are also numerous examples in the Old Testament of how God intervened to forgive and deliver people.

Ahab was considered one of the worst kings who ever reigned in the nation of Israel because he did so much evil. This is how the Old Testament characterizes him: "Now Ahab the son of Omri did evil in the sight of the LORD, more than all who *were* before him" (1 Kings 16:30). If that was not bad enough, he married a woman named Jezebel, "the daughter of Ethbaal, king of the Sidonians." She played an important role in Ahab's wicked reputation. This could have been the epitaph on Ahab's tombstone: "But there was no one like Ahab who sold himself to do wickedness in the sight of the LORD, because Jezebel his wife stirred him up" (21:25). According to verse 29, Ahab finally "humbled himself" before God. As a result, God did not bring or allow any more troubles for the nation in Ahab's days.

I share this story to make this point: Some believe the Old Testament God is an unforgiving God, while the God in the New Testament is forgiving and merciful. When one studies the whole Bible in its context, we will find out it is the same God who is the compassionate Savior in both the Old and New Testaments. "Jesus Christ the same yesterday, and today, and forever" (Heb. 13:8).

Another example is that while Ahab reigned in the northern kingdom of Israel, Manasseh reigned in the southern kingdom of Judah. Manasseh was a cruel tyrant. He was an idolater who turned against God and toward every kind of pagan deity. He is described in the same terms as was his counterpart in the northern kingdom. The story of Manasseh is even more compelling than that of Ahab in showing the love and mercy of God in the Old Testament.

"Manasseh *was* twelve years old when he became king, and he reigned fifty-five years in Jerusalem. His mother's name was Hephzibah. And he did evil in the sight of the LORD, according to the abominations of the nations whom the LORD had cast out before the children of Israel" (2 Kings 21:1, 2).

The passage later recounts just some of Manasseh's wicked works:

> And he built altars for all the host of heaven in the two courts of the house of the LORD. Also, he made his son pass through the fire, practiced soothsaying, used witchcraft, and consulted spiritists and mediums. He did much evil in the sight of the LORD, to provoke *Him* to anger. He even set a carved image of Asherah that he had made, in the house of which the LORD had said to David and to Solomon his son, "In this house and in Jerusalem,

which I have chosen out of all the tribes of Israel, I will put My name forever. (2 Kings 21:5–7)

The end of the reign of Manasseh is recorded this way: "So Manasseh rested with his fathers, and was buried in the garden of his own house, in the garden of Uzza. Then his son Amon reigned in his place" (verse 18).

Now, reading only 2 Kings, one would think the story of Manasseh was over. It is only as we read the parallel version of his story in 2 Chronicles that we learn "the rest of the story" about the life and death of Manasseh. Most importantly, it is in this book that one can make a most compelling case for God's forgiving grace and mercy in the Old Testament.

It is only in the parallel account that we learn "The LORD spoke to Manasseh and his people, but they would not listen. Therefore, the LORD brought upon them the captains of the army of the king of Assyria, who took Manasseh with hooks, bound him with bronze *fetters*, and carried him off to Babylon" (2 Chron. 33:10, 11). God had given the wicked king many opportunities to repent, but he did not. God finally allowed Manasseh's enemy to haul him into exile by taking him to a foreign land. Nevertheless, the mercy of God shone even brighter. While Manasseh was confined to prison in Babylon:

> He implored the LORD his God, and humbled himself greatly before the God of his fathers, and prayed to Him; and He received his entreaty, heard his supplication, and brought him back to Jerusalem into his kingdom. Then Manasseh knew that the LORD *was* God. After this he built a wall outside the City of David on the west side of Gihon, in the valley, as far as the entrance of the Fish Gate; and *it* enclosed Ophel, and he raised it to a very great height. Then he put military captains in all the fortified cities of Judah. He took away the foreign gods and the idol from the house of the LORD, and all the altars that he had built in the mount of the house of the LORD and in Jerusalem; and he cast *them* out of the city. He also repaired the altar of the LORD, sacrificed peace offerings and thank offerings on it, and commanded Judah to serve the LORD God of Israel. (2 Chron. 33:12–16)

The Bible teaches that no matter what sin we have committed, "If we confess our sins, [God] is faithful and just to forgive us our sins, and to cleanse us from all unrighteousness" (1 John 1:9). This is grace in truth! As one continues to read both the Old and New Testaments, one benefits from these stories and receives a more complete picture of what God is like.

CHAPTER 6

REASONING WITH GOD PREMATURELY

In my studies, I have found God to be absolutely reasonable. He loves His creation and is merciful and fair with us. The so-called "other gods" are demanding, cruel, and unreasonable. Here is the language one prophet employs to characterize the true God: "'Come now, and let us reason together,' Says the LORD, 'Though your sins are like scarlet, They shall be as white as snow; Though they are red like crimson, They shall be as wool'" (Isa. 1:18).

What a wonderful, reassuring, heartwarming, blessed promise! Based on this one singular verse, it appears that God is always ready to have communion and fellowship with us—but not so fast! Most of God's promises are conditional. There is a preamble and prerequisite, if you will, to this promise, or else we will misunderstand this and other awesome promises of God in the Bible. You see, despite our assertions to the contrary, there exist inside all of us character traits that disqualify us from receiving a number of His blessings.

Before we come to God to claim certain blessings, we need to give Him the permission to release His powers in us. We must allow God to convert us first, and then He can prepare us to receive these blessings. We are perplexed when our prayers appear to go unanswered. When we pray to God, there are often three possible answers: He says, "Yes" to some requests, "No" to others, especially if it is a request that our wise, compassionate God knows is not good for His children. At other times, God will say, "Wait."

Many of our prayers are not answered because our hearts are not right with God. We need to pray that God will prepare our hearts by helping us repent of our sins. We need to be ready before we can have an intimate relationship with the Almighty. We know He is prepared and willing to pour out His abundant blessings on His people. With that said, why are His blessings withheld for an extended period of time sometimes? This question is answered by the same prophet: "Behold, the LORD's hand is not shortened, That it cannot save; Nor His ear heavy, That it cannot hear. But your iniquities have separated you from your God; And your sins have hidden *His* face from you, So that He will not hear" (59:1, 2).

There we have it. An unconfessed sin builds a wall or chasm between God and us.

> Hear the word of the LORD, You rulers of Sodom; Give ear to the law of our God You people of Gomorrah: "To what purpose *is* the multitude of your sacrifices to Me?" Says the LORD. "I have had enough of burnt offerings of rams And the fat of fed cattle. I do not delight in the blood of bulls, Or of lambs or goats. When you come to appear before Me, Who has required this from your hand, To trample My courts? Bring no more futile sacrifices; Incense is an abomination to Me. The New Moons, the Sabbaths, and the calling of assemblies—I cannot endure iniquity and the sacred meeting. Your New Moons and your appointed feasts My soul hates; They are a trouble to Me, I am weary of bearing *them*. When you spread out your hands, I will hide My eyes from you; Even though you make many prayers, I will not hear. Your hands are full of blood. Wash yourselves, make yourselves clean; Put away the evil of your doings from before My eyes. Cease to do evil, Learn to do good; Seek justice, Rebuke the oppressor; Defend the fatherless, Plead for the widow." (Isa. 1:10–17)

We cannot be self-centered, bigoted, impatient, and cruel toward our fellow human beings and then, with unconsecrated lips and hearts, dare to approach the Holy God. We cannot pray to Him to bless us while we are holding grudges in our hearts toward other people. It is only after we have allowed God to give us converted hearts that these conditions will have been fulfilled and we will be in the position to come and reason with our Maker.

CHAPTER 7

WHAT IS SIN?

I finally found the true definition of "sin" from the Bible. Many flippantly talk about sin without really understanding its true significance or outcome. The Bible's premier definition of sin is "Whosoever committeth *sin* transgresseth also the *law*: for *sin* is the *transgression* of the *law*" (1 John 3:4, KJV, emphasis added). The New Revised Standard Version renders it this way: "Everyone who commits sin is guilty of lawlessness; sin is lawlessness."

Furthermore, the Bible attaches a price for sin. Sin is costly. "For the wages of sin *is* death, but the gift of God *is* eternal life in Christ Jesus our Lord" (Rom. 6:23, NKJV). While it's costly to commit sin, thanks be to God, the same text states that He gives us a gift: eternal life. God knew we never could pay for our sins. Therefore, He gave us eternal life as a gift if we are willing to accept it. It does not mean that because God gives us the gift of eternal life, it is not costly. While the gift of God is free to us, it is very costly to Him. It cost Him the death of His Son, our Lord and Savior, Jesus Christ.

When I learned what this verse was saying, I began to appreciate more what Jesus really did for me when He hung on the cross on Calvary. Instead of living superficially, without any thought of accountability or consequences for my actions, I began to be more circumspect in the way I live.

It makes more sense to me, now, why we need to confess our sins and be converted and washed by the blood of Jesus before we can be in right standing with the Holy God. Why did I used to be so confused? It is because I grew up listening to preachers delivering mixed messages about sin, death, hell, God's forgiveness, and the gift of eternal life. These same preachers told me I needed to repent of my sins, which meant I had broken God's law, or else I would end up in hell. They were the very same preachers who told me, from the other side of their mouths, that "Jesus had done away with the Law of God." Reader, if you have never heard such nonsense from a preacher, you are blessed!

I once inquired of one of these double-tongued teachers/preachers, "Why are you giving this dual message?" He pointed me to Romans 3:20: "Therefore by the deeds of the law no flesh will be justified in His sight, for by the law *is* the knowledge of sin."

I have no problem with this verse. The Bible is clear, and this verse is plain to me. My problem is with the explanation of many preachers and Bible teachers. We are not saved by keeping the Ten Commandments. The purpose of the Ten Commandments is to point out our sins and lead us to Jesus, who is the only One who can save us.

However, the above verse says more than that. While the Ten Commandments cannot save or justify us, if they were removed or abolished, how would we know what sin is? Notwithstanding what I was taught, I found in the same Bible answers for my dilemma. It is inconceivable that the same Ten Commandments that convict and reveal to us that we are sinners and in need of a Savior would be done away with by the Lord Jesus Christ, who gave us the Ten Commandments in the first place.

> **It is inconceivable that the same Ten Commandments that convict and reveal to us that we are sinners and in need of a Savior would be done away with by the Lord Jesus Christ, who gave us the Ten Commandments in the first place.**

It is always a good study practice to read the whole passage in the Bible for context and understanding instead of just one or two verses out of context to try to make a point. "But now the righteousness of God apart from the law is revealed, being witnessed by the Law and the Prophets, even the righteousness of God, through faith in Jesus Christ, to all and on all who believe. For there is no difference; for all have sinned and fall short of the glory of God" (verses 21–23).

The above texts are also clear. We are justified by "the righteousness of God through faith in Jesus Christ." This justification is free "by His grace… through the redemption that is in Jesus Christ." The texts say nothing about Jesus doing away with His Ten Commandments. The only law that was abolished was the ceremonial law that pointed to Jesus as the Redeemer. In fact, Jesus gives the definitive rebuttal to the charge that He had done away with His own Law:

> Do not think that I came to destroy the Law or the Prophets. I did not come to destroy but to fulfill. For assuredly, I say to you, till heaven and earth pass away, one jot or one tittle will by no means pass from the law till all

is fulfilled. Whoever therefore breaks one of the least of these commandments, and teaches men so, shall be called least in the kingdom of heaven; but whoever does and teaches *them,* he shall be called great in the kingdom of heaven. For I say to you, that unless your righteousness exceeds *the righteousness* of the scribes and Pharisees, you will by no means enter the kingdom of heaven. (Matt. 5:17–20)

Jesus' exposition on this topic is so clear that only the enemy, the rebel angel from heaven, could have manufactured such a misunderstanding and false teaching of the book of Romans. Read again what the Lord Jesus Christ said, that whoever breaks "the least of these commandments, and teaches men" to do the same "shall be called least in the kingdom of heaven." In contrast, "whoever does and teaches *them,* he shall be called great in the kingdom of heaven."

Can any teaching by Jesus Himself be clearer? We must keep the Ten Commandments of God, not as a means of salvation, but as evidence of salvation. When we are forgiven and saved by the righteousness of Jesus Christ, we will love Him so much that we will gladly obey Him. His love, grace, and power facilitate that outcome. Elsewhere, the beloved apostle quoted the very words of Jesus to make this point another way: "If you love Me, keep My commandments" (John 14:15).

After Jesus had forgiven a woman caught in adultery, He sent her away by commanding her to "go, and sin no more" (8:11). We have already learned that "sin is the transgression of the law." How foolish it would have been for Jesus to have told this woman to go and sin no more if He had done away with the only mechanism (the Ten Commandments) that would point out and explain to the woman what sin is! Neither this woman nor any one of us has the power to keep God's commandments. However, when He commands us to keep His commandments, it is understood that He will give us the power and strength to obey them. And the best motivation to keep God's commandments is not to gain His favor but because we love Him.

Furthermore, the Bible says we do not even have the motivation to repent of our sins. It is God alone who gives us that ability:

Or do you despise the riches of His goodness, forbearance, and longsuffering, not knowing that the goodness of God leads you to repentance? But in accordance with your hardness and your impenitent heart you are treasuring up for yourself wrath in the day of wrath and revelation of the righteous judgment of God, who 'will render to each one according to his deeds:' eternal life to those who by patient continuance in doing good seek for glory, honor, and immortality; but to those who are self-seeking and do not obey the truth, but obey unrighteousness—indignation and wrath. (Rom. 2:4-8)

This passage warns us not to have hard, impenitent hearts. If we harden our hearts and obey unrighteousness—if we are "impenitent," "self-seeking," and do not obey the truth in the "righteous judgment of God"—we will experience His wrath. Do not despair, dear reader. The good news, as we have seen, is that Jesus died to give us eternal life when we accept Him as our personal Savior and Lord. The word "lord," in a functional sense, means "someone having power, authority, or influence over us." One of the ways one shows respect to the Lord is to be obedient to Him. And it gets better!

Behold, the days are coming, says the Lord, when I will make a new covenant with the house of Israel and with the house of Judah— not according to the covenant that I made with their fathers in the day *that* I took them by the hand to lead them out of the land of Egypt, My covenant which they broke, though I was a husband to them, says the Lord. But this *is* the covenant that I will make with the house of Israel after those days, says the Lord: I will put My law in their minds, and write it on their hearts; and I will be their God, and they shall be My people. (Jer. 31:31-33)

That promise was not just for the people of ancient Israel. It is for all who choose to love and serve the God of Israel. That is the reason this same passage is quoted in the New Testament for Christians (see Heb. 8:8-10).

You see, under the old covenant, most people believed they were saved by strictly keeping the Ten Commandments by their own strength (even though God didn't intend that). Under the new covenant, on the other hand, God writes His law in our hearts. Since the Ten Commandments are the transcript of God's character, this is another way of saying He writes His own character in our hearts, thereby enabling us to be obedient from love.

Furthermore, Jeremiah said, "No more shall every man teach his neighbor, and every man his brother, saying, 'Know the Lord,' for they all shall know Me, from the least of them to the greatest of them, says the Lord. For I will forgive their iniquity, and their sin I will remember no more" (31:34). The reason no one will have to teach us the law of God is because we will have His law (i.e., character) in our hearts. We will obey God spontaneously, just as do the angels who did not rebel against God or need to be taught these things. They continue to spontaneously obey Him, and we can do the same by His love, grace, and power. May the Lord help us to that end!

CHAPTER 8

SHOPPING FOR DISCOUNTS

We live in a world of people who love a good discount. Who doesn't like a good discount? I have heard people have spent hours, even days, waiting in a store line for good bargains. Several years ago, it was reported that some of those so-called "store buster" escapades had yielded deadly results. There are some states where people have been pushed down and trampled to death in their quest to get a discount. Some would do anything for a discount. Unfortunately, many professed followers of God convey the same attitude when it comes to obeying God's commandments.

God's law is a transcript of His character. God is holy; His law is holy; God is just; His commandments are just; God is good; His commandments are good (see Romans 7:12). Modern humanity has gotten rid of God's Ten Commandments. When we try to do away with His law, we try to do away with God Himself. It is no wonder lawlessness abounds all around the world. Others try to bargain for self-discounts. They refuse the Ten Commandments of God. They prefer "the nine commandments." Isn't that convenient—a ten percent discount?

Another class is not satisfied with just a ten percent discount. They prefer a twenty percent discount or more. They pick and choose from God's Ten Commandments what they prefer or find convenient for them. Still others want a full discount. If you have been summoned as a witness in a legal matter, you remember going into a court room, putting your left hand on a Bible, and raising your right hand. A bailiff then asked, "Do you solemnly swear to tell the truth, the whole truth, and nothing but the truth, so help you God?" Don't gloss over the part about putting your left hand on the Bible—the same Bible that contains God's Ten Commandments.

In the early 2000s, this story was filed in Montgomery, Alabama. The state's judicial ethics panel removed Alabama Chief Justice Roy Moore. Judge Moore wanted to keep a Ten Commandments monument in the Alabama Judicial Building. Here is how one of the news outlets reported it:

> Montgomery, Alabama (CNN) -- Alabama's judicial ethics panel removed Chief Justice Roy Moore from office Thursday for defying a federal judge's order to move a Ten Commandments monument from the state Supreme Court building.
>
> The nine-member Court of the Judiciary issued its unanimous decision after a one-day trial Wednesday.
>
> The panel, which includes judges, lawyers and non-lawyers, could have reprimanded Moore, continued his suspension, or cleared him.
>
> The ethics panel said Moore put himself above the law by "willfully and publicly" flouting the order to remove the 2.6-ton monument from the state judicial building's rotunda in August.
>
> U.S. District Judge Myron Thompson ruled the granite carving was an unconstitutional endorsement of religion. Moore refused to obey the order but was overruled by his eight colleagues on the state Supreme Court.
>
> On November 3, 2003, the U.S. Supreme Court refused to hear Moore's appeal of Thompson's ruling.
>
> Moore "showed no signs of contrition for his actions," the Court of the Judiciary found.
>
> Moore's critics said they were not yet satisfied.
>
> Richard Cohen, a lawyer for the Southern Poverty Law Center -- one of the groups that sued Moore over the monument -- said the organization would seek to have Moore disbarred....
>
> Pryor filed the ethics charges after Moore refused to remove the monument.
>
> "God has chosen this time and this place so we can save our country and save our courts for our children," Moore said.
>
> President Bush has nominated Pryor to a seat on the 11th U.S. Circuit Court of Appeals. Senate Democrats are trying to block the nomination by filibuster.
>
> Pryor, a Republican, has said he believes the Ten Commandments display was constitutional, but he said Thursday federal court orders must be obeyed.
>
> "At the end of the day, when the courts resolve those controversies, we respect their decision," he said. "That does not mean that we always agree with their decision."

...With Thompson threatening to fine the state $5,000 a day for defying his order, [Alabama Attorney General Bill] Pryor and Gov. Bob Riley refused to back Moore.

[Both men are fellow] Republican[s] and self-professed conservative Christians who supported the monument's installation, but [Riley] said Moore was bound to obey Thompson's order. (CNN, https://1ref.us/237, [accessed Sept. 28, 2022])

My interest in this story is not the position a secular jurist takes but how professed Christians are dealing with God's law. Sometimes, an incident or story may at first appear to be clear cut, only to become unraveled out of proportion until one is left scratching one's head and saying, "I am not sure what to believe anymore."

I included this story in this chapter to make several points. First, think about this question: How do you punish a judge for displaying in a courthouse the Ten Commandments, which are used to compel people to swear to tell the truth? By the way, the commandment to tell the truth is the ninth commandment: "You shall not bear false witness against your neighbor" (Exod. 20:16). In other words, you shall not lie, but tell the truth.

Second, the judge was not punished by "heathens" in a faraway, atheistic country. He was punished in beautiful America, the land of the free, amid a people whose motto is "In God we trust." Furthermore, according to the article, Judge Moore was punished, in part, by fellow "conservative Christians." I'll let this point speak for itself.

Finally, this story reminds me of another one. In this Bible story, a couple of Jesus' disciples were summoned to a religious panel or "council." They were accused of disobeying an order not to preach the gospel of the resurrected Christ. You may be familiar with the story, but please indulge me as I quote a few lines:

And when they had brought [the disciples], they set *them* before the council. And the high priest asked them, saying, "Did we not strictly command you not to teach in this name? And look, you have filled Jerusalem with your doctrine, and intend to bring this Man's blood on us!" But Peter and the *other* apostles answered and said: "We ought to obey God rather than men. (Acts 5:27–29)

Yes, there are still a few good people in the world who still obey God rather than mankind!

Why is the truth so difficult to see? It is because we live, as it were, in a sea mixed with truth and error—so-called "situation ethics." Our society—the whole culture—is built and maintained by half-truths or outright deception. Many professed Christians feel they must follow "the norm" of society or else they will not fit in or succeed in the world. Even those who outwardly appear to be zealous about spiritual things, advocating moral issues and high ideals such as democracy, tolerance, pro-life, and anti-homosexuality, do the filthiest activities privately—behind closed doors.

> Why is the truth so difficult to see? It is because we live, as it were, in a sea mixed with truth and error—so-called "situation ethics."

Despite their denial to the contrary, they easily manipulate or "spin" the truth. When God's directives are presented, they quickly find excuses as to why they are right. On the other hand, while they reject any obligation to do what is right, they advocate a certain view, then quickly find a way to excuse themselves from any responsibility.

Therefore, it requires each one of us who professes to be a citizen of the kingdom of God to resist rationalizing falsehood. We need to "swim against the tide," if you will, to truly live as citizens of His kingdom. We are here on earth on probation. I believe we are being observed by the angels of heaven to see if we hold the truth in a consistent way, not merely when it is convenient. Like our forefather Abraham, we are to live here on earth while at the same time looking "for the city which has foundations, whose builder and maker *is* God" (Heb. 11:10).

Beloved, let us not live callously and think we are safe, even in a religious nation such as "America the Beautiful." Our only safeguard is to know Jesus and follow His example from His Word, the Bible. We must pray like we have never prayed before and follow Jesus' counsel, "Then Jesus said to those Jews who believed Him, 'If you abide in My word, you are My disciples indeed. And you shall know the truth, and the truth shall make you free'" (John 8:31, 32).

The enemy of God has redoubled his efforts to do away with the Ten Commandments, which are our only safeguard against total chaos and anarchy in the world. Satan's plan has succeeded in most parts of the world. Now freedom-loving America is in his sights. It is the duty of all God's loving people to remain faithful to Him by the power of the Holy Spirit.

CHAPTER 9

LET THE CARPENTER BUILD HIS TEMPLE

There is a story preachers use to illustrate Jesus working on behalf of people. It goes this way: Once upon a time, two brothers lived on adjoining farms. John, the older, and James, the younger, had a terrible fight. The relationship began to fall apart over a small misunderstanding. Harsh words were exchanged until finally, their relationship was severely broken.

One morning, there was a knock at John's door. He opened it to find a shabby little man with an ancient carpenter's toolbox. "I'm looking for a few days of work," he said. "Perhaps you have a few small jobs here that I could help you with?"

"Yes," said John, "I do have a job for you. Look across the creek at that farm. That's my younger brother's place. Some time ago, there was a meadow between us, but he took his bulldozer to it, and now there is a creek. He did this to spite me, but I'll do him even better. See that pile of lumber by the barn? I want you to build an eight-foot fence so that I won't see his face, or place, ever again."

The carpenter said, "I'll do the best job that I can to meet your satisfaction." John helped the carpenter get ready, and then he was off for the day.

The carpenter worked hard all that day, measuring, sawing, and nailing. When John returned at sunset, the carpenter had just finished his job. John's jaw dropped. There was no fence! Instead, the carpenter had built a bridge that stretched from one side of the creek to the other. It was a beautiful piece of work, with handrails and all. John's brother, James, crossed the bridge and, with tears in his eyes, hugged his older brother.

"John, you're a better man than I am to build this bridge after all that I have said and done." The happy brothers turned to see the carpenter hoisting his toolbox onto his shoulder."

John said, "No, wait! Please, stay a few days. I have a lot of other projects for you."

"Thank you, I'd love to stay," said the carpenter, "but there are so many more bridges still to be built."

We are living in a time when multitudes of people do not want to learn about God's ways. They feel the "Carpenter of Nazareth" interferes too much with their plans and desires. Many, if not most, prefer another type of "carpenter" to work in their lives. The world-loving heart has rejected the admonition of the Lord. Satan is all too ready to provide another builder. He supplies many deceptions to fit their world-loving hearts. Life is measured by the latest result of a Gallop poll, the latest experiment, the decision of the U.S. Supreme Court, or the verdict of a jury.

While each has its proper sphere, God's opinion should matter most. We are no different from the people in the Bible. Most of them "did their own thing" regardless of what God said. "Every man did what was right in his own eyes" (Judges 21:25, RSV). This is a good time to let Jesus build His temple in us, which the Bible says figuratively we are.

Jesus had a conversation with His disciples. He told them how He would be killed by the rulers of Israel. Jesus' disciples protested. "Then Peter took Him aside and began to rebuke Him, saying, 'Far be it from You, Lord; this shall not happen to You!'" (Matt. 16:22). Imagine a disciple rebuking his Lord. Imagine Jesus' own disciple not understanding His mission. This is the result of having one's own agenda.

The people in Jesus' day expected a king who would destroy the Roman power and reign as king. Jesus had another agenda and mission. His mission was to deliver people from sin, not from the Romans. We must let Jesus teach and guide us into His truth. He wants His followers to choose peace, not war. Otherwise, evil angels will so blind our minds and harden our hearts that we shall not be impressed by God's truth. Satan adapts his temptations to all classes. He will find a way to infiltrate the believer who does not allow Jesus to lead his or her life.

> Satan adapts his temptations to all classes. He will find a way to infiltrate the believer who does not allow Jesus to lead his or her life.

The Bible compares the Christian's body to a building—a temple, if you will. God's desire is to dwell in that temple. "And that He might reconcile them both to God in one body through the cross, thereby putting to death the enmity. And He came and preached peace to you who were afar off and to those who were near" (Eph. 2:16, 17).

Therefore, the Lord wants to dwell in the real temple, which is one's heart. "Or do you not know that your body is the temple of the Holy Spirit *who is* in you, whom you have from God, and you are not your own?" (1 Cor. 6:19). Because we are not our own, it behooves us to live our lives very carefully. We are to glorify God in our bodies by allowing the Holy Spirit to dwell therein.

The Lord wants to dwell in a clean, surrendered heart, but that won't be possible if we do not allow Jesus to first clean and rebuild the temple correctly. If we refuse to let God into our hearts, the heart-temple remains unclean because only the Holy Spirit can cleanse the heart. When we accept the Lord Jesus Christ into our hearts, we become the temple of God through the Holy Spirit, who dwells in us.

We are to be very vigilant in what we put into the temple of God. We also need to watch how we conduct our lives in this subtly perilous world. We should not live our lives as if they were just a matter of chance. The Bible cautions us with this precise message: "Unless the Lord builds the house, they labor in vain who build it; unless the Lord guards the city, the watchman stays awake in vain" (Ps. 127:1). The Lord is very purposeful and intentional toward those whom He rules, and we should also live our lives with His purpose and intent.

The previous verse means more than building an ordinary edifice. As we have seen, the Bible says we, God's people, are the temple of the Holy Spirit. If we do not allow the Spirit to construct a holy dwelling in our hearts—if we insist on building our own lives—our work will collapse, and we will make a ruin of our lives.

To help illustrate the above point, let us consider these two scenarios: First, suppose you are a builder constructing a house. You spend an enormous amount of time and money on the project. After the work is completed, a storm comes and destroys the house completely. Second, you are a sentry guarding an important building. Unbeknown to you, there is an enemy who is lurking not too far away. Before you can react, the enemy overcomes you and seizes the property. These two scenarios are bad enough in themselves, but imagine if either of these examples depicts the status of your soul.

How do we surrender and allow Jesus into our lives to build us correctly? We need to understand that before God asks us to seek Him, He is already at work for us. Listen to these words as you read: God "has saved us, and called us with an holy calling, not according to our works, but according to his own purpose and grace, which was given us in Christ Jesus before the world began" (2 Tim. 1:9). Please do not miss this implication. Even before we were born—

even before we acknowledged Him—God had a plan to save us through His Son, Jesus Christ. All that remains is for us to surrender and let Jesus be in charge.

Psalm 127:1 cautions us: If God is not in charge of building our spiritual lives, we are erecting houses that will soon collapse by a terrible flood. In other words, if He is not the Guardian of the soul, some unexpected enemy will seize it. The enemy will take control of our hearts and wreak havoc on our souls. This is the reason we should surrender our lives to the Master Builder. Give Him the blueprints of our lives and let Him build them from beginning to end. How do we find God to allow Him to do this work for us? "And you will seek Me and find *Me,* when you search for Me with all your heart" (Jer. 29:13).

Let us consider another promise from God's Word: "And we know that all things work together for good to those who love God, to those who are the called according to *His* purpose" (Rom. 8:28). This promise assures us that no matter what we are experiencing in this life, if we search for God and surrender our lives to Him, we will be safe in His hands. He has already ordained our victory. This is a certainty! God keeps His promises.

Furthermore, when we face challenging times and obstacles, it does not mean God is not with us. It could simply mean He is strengthening us to be able to endure more difficult tests ahead. He is just building and preparing His temple in which He will dwell.

CHAPTER 10

MISTAKEN ZEAL

Paul said about the people of Israel, "Brethren, my heart's desire and prayer to God for Israel is that they may be saved. For I bear them witness that they have a zeal for God, but not according to knowledge. For they being ignorant of God's righteousness, and seeking to establish their own righteousness, have not submitted to the righteousness of God" (Rom. 10:1–3).

We are to be careful not to substitute our own ideas, biases, and feelings for God's. We cannot work for the Lord in our own power. It is imperative that we surrender ourselves daily to Jesus. He is the Vine; we are the branches; without Him, we can do nothing, especially in terms of being faithful disciples. Again, zeal for the Lord and His cause is wonderful, but our zeal must be under the lordship of Jesus Christ. We may have done important things for God, but there are momentous events that need to take place, both in the world and in our lives, before Jesus returns. His followers should have a different experience—a different spirit.

There are many religious people today who have taken upon themselves the task to push a "Jesus agenda" in secular governments or courts. They want to have prayer restored in schools or other public institutions. Many of these well-intentioned folks have seen the deterioration of society and feel like they must try to do something about it. On the surface, this sounds very noteworthy and even pious, but a close, careful examination of these efforts would find them to be very deceptive and dangerous.

First, the Lord never gave his followers such an assignment. Jesus' most important command to His followers is to "Go into all the world and preach the gospel to every creature" (Mark 16:15). The Lord knows only the preaching of the gospel by the Holy Spirit has the power to change the hearts of sinful men and women. No human laws in the name of an executive, legislative, or judicial body or any earthly government will initiate true, lasting spiritual transformation.

Second, a cursory examination of history will reveal that all such efforts in the past have yielded horrifying religious persecutions to the tune of untold millions of lost lives. In fact, it is evidence of spiritual bankruptcy when religious leaders and their followers must resort to a civil government to enforce their dogmas. They chose to neglect the sanctifying power of the Holy Spirit in their lives. These leaders, being intoxicated with the "wine of Babylon," enact the only natural, depraved result of doing the work of their cruel, wicked master, Satan. In fact, these types of religious persecutions will get worse just prior to the second coming of Christ.

The disciples of Jesus were exuberant as He made His triumphant entry into Jerusalem. They were rejoicing because they thought Jesus was finally going to exalt Himself as king. They believed He was now ready to rule in His Davidic kingdom. "Therefore, when Jesus perceived that they were about to come and take Him by force to make Him king, He departed again to the mountain by Himself alone" (John 6:15).

However, Jesus said to Pilate, the Roman governor, and subsequently to all who believed He must rule a human kingdom, "My kingdom is not of this world. If My kingdom were of this world, My servants would fight, so that I should not be delivered to the Jews; but now My kingdom is not from here" (18:36) This was something profound to ponder by all who wanted to push Jesus into the forefront of their political agenda. And in meditating on His words, we can learn an insightful principle for how to be ready and equipped to engage in service—the true service that God alone will empower us to do.

We have prayed "without ceasing" that we would not be deceived into doing the work of the archfiend. God will do His own work—the work we cannot do. "Being confident of this very thing, that He who has begun a good work in you will complete *it* until the day of Jesus Christ" (Phil. 1:6).

We would do well to remember another story from the Bible involving the sons of Aaron. "Then Nadab and Abihu, the sons of Aaron, each took his censer and put fire in it, put incense on it, and offered profane fire before the Lord, which He had not commanded them. So, fire went out from the Lord and devoured them, and they died before the Lord" (Lev. 10:1, 2). These two priests had become intoxicated and forgotten the commandment of God. It is obvious that the Lord was not pleased with these men. Although they were religious men, they "served" Him with their own depraved minds.

Another sad, tragic incident in the Bible about good intentions going terribly wrong is when the Philistines captured the ark of the covenant. The story started with a prophet of God named Eli. "Now the sons of Eli *were* corrupt; they did not know the LORD" (1 Sam. 2:12). The nation of Israel had gone to war with its old enemy, the Philistines, who had just routed Israel that day. The elders of Israel thought they had lost because they had not taken the ark of the covenant into the battle.

Eli's corrupt sons, Hophni and Phinehas, did not know the Lord. They took the ark into battle with them. These sons and the elders thought of the ark as a lucky charm—not treating it with the dignity and respect it deserved. Things deteriorated. "Also, the ark of God was captured; and the two sons of Eli, Hophni and Phinehas, died" (4:11). The incident became even more heartbreaking. On the same day, when the news of this tragedy reached the ears of the elderly Eli, he fell backward from his seat, broke his neck, and died.

When the people of Ashdod, a city in Philistia, concluded it was too dangerous for them to keep the ark, they passed it first to Gath, then to another place called Ekron. The people of Ekron refused to keep it. After consulting with the Philistine priests, they decided to promptly return the ark back to Israel. The Philistines had kept the ark for seven months. The advice of the priests of the Philistines are chronicled as follows:

"Now therefore, make a new cart, take two milk cows which have never been yoked, and hitch the cows to the cart; and take their calves home, away from them. Then take the ark of the LORD and set it on the cart; and put the articles of gold which you are returning to Him *as* a trespass offering in a chest by its side. Then send it away, and let it go. And watch: if it goes up the road to its own territory, to Beth Shemesh, *then* He has done us this great evil. But if not, then we shall know that *it is* not His hand *that* struck us—it happened to us by chance." Then the men did so; they took two milk cows and hitched them to the cart, and shut up their calves at home. And they set the ark of the LORD on the cart... Then the cows headed straight for the road to Beth Shemesh, *and* went along the highway, lowing as they went, and did not turn aside to the right hand or the left. And the lords of the Philistines went after them to the border of Beth Shemesh.... Then He struck the men of Beth Shemesh, because they had looked into the ark of the LORD. (1 Sam. 6:7–12, 19)

The ark ended up in the home of a priest named Abinadab for twenty years. After David had become the king of Israel, he decided to bring the ark from the house of Abinadab to his own city, Jerusalem. A new cart was built, and the ark was placed on it. Uzzah and Ahio, the sons of Abinadab, drove the new cart.

> And they brought it out of the house of Abinadab, which *was* on the hill, accompanying the ark of God; and Ahio went before the ark. Then David and all the house of Israel played *music* before the Lord on all kinds of *instruments of* fir wood, on harps, on stringed instruments, on tambourines, on sistrums, and on cymbals. And when they came to Nachon's threshing floor, Uzzah put out *his hand* to the ark of God and took hold of it, for the oxen stumbled. Then the anger of the Lord was aroused against Uzzah, and God struck him there for *his* error; and he died there by the ark of God. (2 Sam. 6:4–7)

David was furious that the Lord had struck down Uzzah. Even the king did not fully grasp the magnitude of the action. What was the great error of Uzzah? After all, he was simply trying to prevent the ark from tumbling to the ground.

We get the first clue to this serious consequence in Numbers 4:14–15. The Lord had commanded the Kohathites, a specific group of Levites, to transport the special furnishings. They were supposed to carry the poles that were in the rings attached to the wood. The Kohathites were not to touch the sacred furnishings with their bare hands. Forgetting God's directions, they followed the manner of the Philistines by putting the ark on a "new" cart.

> **David was furious that the Lord had struck down Uzzah. Even the king did not fully grasp the magnitude of the action. What was the great error of Uzzah? After all, he was simply trying to prevent the ark from tumbling to the ground.**

God made it perfectly clear that He does not accept unconsecrated ways of worshipping Him, nor are we to take it upon ourselves to change His directives. Consequently, when we deal with the commandments of God, we are to make sure we do not change, add to, or remove even an iota from them. God requires us to observe His rules in whatever we try to do for Him. David had finally learned the proper way to carry the ark. He was successful in bringing it to Jerusalem the second time when the priests and he had followed God's directions.

We are often told we are now living in a "new" dispensation. "These specific instructions are not sacred anymore." "They are not valid any longer." We make "new carts" for ourselves to force people to adhere to our interpreted dogmas. We follow the examples we see in other churches to satisfy God's instructions. We reason that this will attract more people to our congregations and we will have bigger offerings. That is how we rationalize and offer "strange fire" on the altar of God.

We are not to use tactics God has not ordained. Just because our merciful Lord does not strike us down as He did Uzzah, we should not continue "business as usual." We would do well to remember what a wise man wrote long ago:

> Because the sentence against an evil work is not executed speedily, therefore the heart of the sons of men is fully set in them to do evil. Though a sinner does evil a hundred *times,* and his *days* are prolonged, yet I surely know that it will be well with those who fear God, who fear before Him. But it will not be well with the wicked; nor will he prolong *his* days, *which are* as a shadow, because he does not fear before God. (Eccles. 8:11–13)

We cannot, without dire consequences, follow the maxims of humanity—the church of the Philistines. "Can a man take fire to his bosom, and his clothes not be burned? Can one walk on hot coals, and his feet not be seared?" (Prov. 6:27, 28).

Someone has said, "There is nothing wrong with having zeal in doing God's work. But we have to make sure that our zeal is not one that is mistaken. We must do God's work His way and not our way."

CHAPTER 11

PSEUDO JUDGES

In this chapter, I will share some passages from the Holy Bible that have taught me lessons about true and false judgments. Let me start with why we should not "judge" others. These are the words of Jesus: "Judge not, that you be not judged. For with what judgment you judge, you will be judged; and with the measure you use, it will be measured back to you. And why do you look at the speck in your brother's eye, but do not consider the plank in your own eye?" (Matt. 7:1–3). This does not mean we should not use discernment. Moments later, Jesus himself said, "By their fruit we shall know them" (verse 16).

We need to consider the situation and use good judgment when we examine the fruit of others and ourselves to see whether it is good or bad. When Jesus said we should not judge, it means we should not *condemn* others. Judging is God's job. Furthermore, Jesus, when referring to judging, is talking to hypocrites who condemn others while they themselves are doing the same thing or even worse.

Here is another passage to warn hypocrites about condemning others:

Therefore you are inexcusable, O man, whoever you are who judge, for in whatever you judge another you condemn yourself; for you who judge practice the same things. But we know that the judgment of God is according to truth against those who practice such things. And do you think this, O man, you who judge those practicing such things, and doing the same, that you will escape the judgment of God? Or do you despise the riches of His goodness, forbearance, and longsuffering, not knowing that the goodness of God leads you to repentance? But in accordance with your hardness and your impenitent heart you are treasuring up for yourself wrath in the day of wrath and revelation of the righteous judgment of God, who "will render to each one according to his deeds": eternal life to those who by patient continuance in doing good seek for glory, honor, and immortality; but to those who are self-seeking and do not obey the truth, but obey unrighteousness—indignation and wrath, tribulation and anguish, on every soul of man who does evil, of the Jew first and also of the Greek; but glory, honor, and peace to everyone who works what is good, to the Jew first and also to the Greek. For there is no partiality with God. (Rom. 2:1–11)

Let us read a couple more passages about judgment being condemned. I share this passage to show how God looks at our hearts and minds, not just at the outside, as most of us do.

The gospel of Luke has two of my favorite lessons from Jesus about how even a person of faith should not condemn someone else. In chapter 12, Jesus was talking to a group of religious people about hypocrisy and why they should not judge others. Some came and told Him about a tragedy that had befallen some Galileans. I must admit I found Jesus reply at that time to be insightful.

There were present at that season some who told Him about the Galileans whose blood Pilate had mingled with their sacrifices. And Jesus answered and said to them, "Do you suppose that these Galileans were worse sinners than all other Galileans, because they suffered such things? I tell you, no; but unless you repent you will all likewise perish." (Luke 13:1–3)

What a rebuke to those of us who love to compare ourselves to those we deem greater sinners than we are! We choose to forget the Bible declares that "all have sinned and come short of the glory of God" (Rom. 3:23).

However, Jesus was not done. He had a bonus in store for self-appointed judges. He continued, "Or those eighteen on whom the tower in Siloam fell and killed them, do you think that they were worse sinners than all other men who dwelt in Jerusalem? I tell you, no; but unless you repent you will all likewise perish" (Luke 13:4, 5).

My friends, I have said it before, but please allow me to say it again. The Bible admonishes us not to compare ourselves with other sinners who "are not wise" (2 Cor. 10:12). Earlier, Paul said, "For who makes you differ from another? And what do you have that you did not receive? Now if you did indeed receive it, why do you boast as if you had not received it?" (1 Cor. 4:7). *The Message* paraphrase of the Bible restates this verse:

For who do you know that really knows *you*, knows your heart? And even if they did, is there anything they would discover in you that you could take credit for? Isn't everything you *have* and everything you *are* sheer gifts from God? So, what's the point of all this comparing and competing? You already have all you need. You already have more access to God than you can handle.

We need that kind of lesson today more than ever!

Another lesson that humbled me is found a little earlier in Luke's account. This one teaches endurance and consistency:

When an unclean spirit goes out of a man, he goes through dry places, seeking rest; and finding none, he says, "I will return to my house from which I came." And when he comes, he finds *it* swept and put in order. Then he goes and takes with *him* seven other spirits more wicked than himself, and they enter and dwell there; and the last *state* of that man is worse than the first. And it happened, as He spoke these things, that a certain woman from the crowd raised her voice and said to Him, "Blessed *is* the womb that bore You, and *the* breasts which nursed You!" But He said, "More than that, blessed *are* those who hear the word of God and keep it!" (Luke 11:24–28, NKJV)

The Contemporary English Version states it this way:

When an evil spirit leaves a person, it travels through the desert, looking for a place to rest. But when it doesn't find a place, it says, "I will go back to the home I left." When it gets there and finds the place clean and fixed up, it goes off and finds seven other evil spirits even worse than itself. They all come and make their home there, and that person ends up in worse shape than before. While Jesus was still talking, a woman in the crowd spoke up, "The woman who gave birth to you and nursed you is blessed!" Jesus replied, "That's true, but the people who are really blessed are the ones who hear and obey God's message!"

One of our biggest dangers is to begin the Christian experience and then allow it to wane after some time. The above story teaches us not to give up once we start on the journey of consecrating our lives to God. Many are emboldened in their wickedness and sinful pleasure. They have no desire to change at all. This story, however, speaks about a person who was willing to change. Regrettably, because he did not endure until the end, "the last state of that man is worse" than it was before he started.

It also teaches us that the devil is a relentless hunter, seeking to ruin our souls, especially as we get closer to the second coming of Christ. The devil never stops his pursuit after us, desiring to leave us in a worse state. We are blessed, though, because the Holy Spirit continues to pursue us with the love of Jesus.

CHAPTER 12

THE HEN AND THE PIG

A humorous parable is told about a chicken and a pig that were walking in front of a restaurant one morning (Many versions of this have been told, but this one is my favorite). There was a sign in front of the restaurant advertising a breakfast special: "Eggs with bacon for $1.99."

The hen said to the pig, "Let us go inside and have breakfast."

The pig answered, "Oh, no, no way, not me."

"Why?" the hen asked.

"Because when we go in there, they will ask you for an offering, but they will ask me for a sacrifice."

Like the pig in this story, we avoid, like the plague, the topics of commitment and sacrifice. We think God is a God who demands too much from us, so we would rather carve out for ourselves an easier life. Jesus says, "For whoever desires to save his life will lose it, but whoever loses his life for My sake will find it" (Matt. 16:25).

Many people shop for churches like they are shopping for a new pair of shoes. We do not like to hear any messages about taking up our cross and following God. "After all," some would insist, "we are saved by grace; we do not have to do anything else." Yet, the above words from Jesus' lips are undeniable. We would do well to examine them more closely. They are relevant for us today who are living in this carefree environment. Jesus added elsewhere, "Come to Me, all *you* who labor and are heavy laden, and I will give you rest. Take My yoke upon you and learn from Me, for I am gentle and lowly in heart, and you will find rest for your souls. For My yoke *is* easy and My burden is light" (11:28–30).

> **Many people shop for churches like they are shopping for a new pair of shoes. We do not like to hear any messages about taking up our cross and following God.**

Allow me to share a new perspective as to why Jesus invites us to take His "yoke" and "burden." At the same time, I will share a few steps on how to take the yoke and burden of Jesus Christ and find true rest and success in this life. Because Jesus said, "Come to me," we should do it. This imperative is from Him whom we profess to follow and should be sufficient for us.

We are to go to Jesus to find solutions to life's perplexing problems. Many who are pondering life's difficult questions would rather go to politicians or radio talk shows for answers. Others would rather go to fortune tellers, gurus, or drug pushers instead of to their Creator and loving Savior. If you need rest from hard work and other heavy burdens, He will give you peace and success.

Jesus said, "Take my yoke upon you." What is His yoke or burden? Whether we like burdens or not, if we are living on earth, they will come. There is the yoke of living under other peoples' expectations; there is the yoke of how people will think of us; there is the yoke of "keeping up with the Joneses"; there is the yoke of fashion; there is the yoke of worrying about being attractive enough; there is the yoke of wanting to be popular; there is the yoke of hoping a person will love and accept us; there is the yoke of having to be "cool."

In other words, we all have our own particular yokes or burdens. Christ's yoke is easy, yet it is still a yoke. The yoke is easy only as we surrender to God daily and are faithful and obedient. For the disobedient, "The way of the transgressor is hard" (Prov. 13:15 KJV; NKJV—"the way of the unfaithful is hard").

The yoke and sacrifice are hard because we are in rebellion against God. The closer we get to Jesus, the easier the yoke and sacrifice will become. I read somewhere that our brains have nerve impulses (neurons) that fire like a line of falling dominoes. This activity is the process that creates the intricate pathway of thought, also called "memory traces" or "neural pathways." The neural pathways create patterns of thought.

Once these pathways are created, the thoughts are likely to be repeated. This is because the repetition of a thought decreases the biochemical resistance to that thought happening again, and the connections between two brain cells on the neural pathway become stronger. With the brain, every time one thinks a thought, the resistance is reduced, therefore increasing the likelihood of one having that thought again. That is how habits are formed.

That is also why learning something new or breaking a habit can be difficult at first. The key is to stick to it. Then it will become easier. Some of the easiest tasks can become difficult when we do not want to do them (washing dishes or doing homework, for example). For us to succeed—to grow spiritually—and to have life eternal—we must learn from Jesus. Besides, He is our example—our pattern—by which we are to live.

Jesus made the supreme sacrifice and bore a heinous yoke to bring life and immortality to us. Our sacrifice is small in comparison to His. When we neglect Bible study and prayer for a long time, it causes us to avoid Christ's yoke. Our minds are not in sync with spiritual things. Therefore, we get bored easily with spiritual things. God wants us to reach the highest standard; and this is manifested through obedience to His precepts.

Another reason Christ's burden is easy has to do with the fact that He is not like other masters. You know about those who sit in the shade sipping lemonade while their servants are toiling in the hot sun. Praise the Lord, Christ is walking next to us with the yoke also around His neck! And when we are too tired to go any further, He puts His strong arm around our waists to carry us forward.

"No temptation has overtaken you except such as is common to man; but God *is* faithful, who will not allow you to be tempted beyond what you are able, but with the temptation will also make the way of escape, that you may be able to bear *it*" (1 Cor. 10:13). Now, this is a promise we can hold very dear in our hearts! Yes, Jesus' yoke is definitely easy. Praise His blessed name!

CHAPTER 13

GOOD AND BAD RELIGIOUS PRACTICES

We live in a world where everything we want to know is at our fingertips. We are overwhelmed with all kinds of information. Yet, one of the most pervasive religious practices is the acceptance and blind following of what others teach about God and the Bible without any serious investigation. We need to be aware of and examine long-established religious traditions that are supposed to be from the Bible. The "old-time religion" needs to be audited very carefully. Many of those old tenets or creeds have nothing to do with biblical faith but are traditions passed down from one generation to another.

While there is legitimacy to passing down "the faith that was once delivered to the saints," we are to test every point for ourselves to see if it is indeed a "Thus saith the Lord." Some of us swallow "hook, line, and sinker" just because the person has a big title after his or her name. The practice of examining for ourselves before we accept a teaching is good Bible religion. Accepting what others say is not just bad religion; it might cause us to lose both our earthly and eternal life.

The Bible admonishes us to "Prove all things; hold fast that which is good" (1 Thess. 5:21). Furthermore, we are encouraged to "examine yourselves, to see whether you are in the faith. Test yourselves. Or do you not realize this about yourselves, that Jesus Christ is in you?—unless indeed you fail to meet the test!" (2 Cor. 13:5 ESV). Had the people in Jesus' day studied the prophesies about Him themselves instead of accepting what their leaders had taught them, fewer would have rejected Him. The practice of blindly following religious leaders has not changed much, even after two millennia. We live in a world where the status quo is good enough for millions. Multitudes believe dogmas simply because of what their religious leaders have taught them.

We need to pass the truth on to our families, friends, and "unto the uttermost parts of the world." However, it must be the truth that is carefully studied and examined. We are to believe and follow truths that are "unto the Lord," not anyone who claims to be from God. Furthermore, what we need to remember is God has no grandchildren. Our parents may have been the most dedicated believers. They lived the truth they knew. God has accepted their sincerity. However, we need to accept God personally—for ourselves—as our Lord and Savior. "The path of the just is as the shining light, that shines more and more unto the perfect day" (Prov. 4:18).

> God has no grandchildren. Our parents may have been the most dedicated believers. They lived the truth they knew. God has accepted their sincerity. However, we need to accept God personally—for ourselves—as our Lord and Savior.

In other words, as we live our lives day by day with God, the road to eternal life will get brighter and brighter. What we study in His Word will be clearer and clearer. We should be better followers of the Lord than our ancestors were, especially as the day of the His coming draws near.

There is another error against which we should guard. The error of going to the opposite extreme has swung the pendulum too far. Some reject religion altogether because of false prophets and teachings. Many reject "organized" religion because of all the atrocities of the past or evil practices in religion today. Their argument is that organized religion is flawed and a sham, and that is putting it mildly. They do not want to join any organized religion. I am sure those who hold these views are not advocating the joining of an "unorganized religion."

The Lord is a very organized Deity. He always has had an organized, small group of people serving Him, even in this polluted, sinful world. In fact, when it comes to spiritual things, the majority is not necessarily right. If you are looking for the largest group as proof of a true religion, you will be most deceived.

Jesus issued a stern warning:

> Enter by the narrow gate; for wide *is* the gate and broad *is* the way that leads to destruction, and there are many who go in by it. Because narrow *is* the

gate and difficult *is* the way which leads to life, and there are few who find it. Beware of false prophets, who come to you in sheep's clothing, but inwardly they are ravenous wolves. You will know them by their fruits. Do men gather grapes from thorn bushes or figs from thistles? Even so, every good tree bears good fruit, but a bad tree bears bad fruit. A good tree cannot bear bad fruit, nor *can* a bad tree bear good fruit. Every tree that does not bear good fruit is cut down and thrown into the fire. Therefore by their fruits you will know them. (Matt. 7:13–20)

We need to earnestly pray that God will lead us to His true people. We should not be satisfied with a part-time, show-and-tell religion, despite how many followers the popular churches boast to have. On the other hand, we cannot just reject religion altogether or casually straddle the line. That is also a very precarious position. Some people just do not want "too much" of God or religion at all. They want just a little, particularly when they are in some danger. The following poem, based on the poem by Wilbur Rees "$3 Worth of God," depicts the attitude of these people:

I would like to buy three dollars worth of God, please…
I would like to buy just a little of the Lord.

Not enough to explode my soul or disturb my sleep,
Not enough to take control of my life; I'll keep

Just enough to equal a cup of warm milk
Just enough to ease some of the pain from my guilt.

I would like to buy three dollars worth of God, please…
Not enough to change my heart; I can only stand

Just enough to take to church when I have the time,
Just enough to equal a snooze in the sunshine.

I want ecstasy, not transformation.
I want the warmth of the womb, but not a new birth…

Not enough to make people see a change in me,
Not enough to impose responsibility…

Just enough to exhibit once a week on Sunday.
I would like to buy three dollars worth of God, please…

You see, before God can lead us and help us with our dilemma in this confused religious sea, we must be willing to surrender all to Him until the end. Even when we do not have all the answers to what we are asking, Jesus says, "He who endures to the end shall be saved" (Matt. 24:13). Keep the faith, dear reader. Do not give up. Our faithful, loving God will lead you safely to your destination.

Daniel is a wonderful example of the persistent entreaty of a godly person amid confusion. He was taken captive to ancient Babylon. Of course, that was because God's people were disobedient and rebellious. Daniel's prayer is worthy of emulation, especially when things are not as clear as we would like. He included himself as he interceded with the Lord for his people. Notice how Daniel used the pronouns "we" and "us" as he offered this heart-moving prayer:

> In the first year of Darius the son of Ahasuerus, of the lineage of the Medes, who was made king over the realm of the Chaldeans— in the first year of his reign I, Daniel, understood by the books the number of the years *specified* by the word of the Lord through Jeremiah the prophet, that He would accomplish seventy years in the desolations of Jerusalem. Then I set my face toward the Lord God to make request by prayer and supplications, with fasting, sackcloth, and ashes. And I prayed to the Lord my God, and made confession, and said, "O Lord, great and awesome God, who keeps His covenant and mercy with those who love Him, and with those who keep His commandments, we have sinned and committed iniquity, we have done wickedly and rebelled, even by departing from Your precepts and Your judgments. Neither have we heeded Your servants the prophets, who spoke in Your name to our kings and our princes, to our fathers and all the people of the land. O Lord, righteousness *belongs* to You, but to us shame of face, as *it is* this day—to the men of Judah, to the inhabitants of Jerusalem and all Israel, those near and those far off in all the countries to which You have driven them, because of the unfaithfulness which they have committed against You. O Lord, to us *belongs* shame of face, to our kings, our princes, and our fathers, because we have sinned against You. To the Lord our God *belong* mercy and forgiveness, though we have rebelled against Him. We have not obeyed the voice of the Lord our God, to walk in His laws, which He set before us by His servants the prophets. Yes, all Israel has transgressed Your law, and has departed so as not to obey Your voice; therefore the curse and

the oath written in the Law of Moses the servant of God have been poured out on us, because we have sinned against Him. And He has confirmed His words, which He spoke against us and against our judges who judged us, by bringing upon us a great disaster; for under the whole heaven such has never been done as what has been done to Jerusalem. As *it is* written in the Law of Moses, all this disaster has come upon us; yet we have not made our prayer before the Lord our God, that we might turn from our iniquities and understand Your truth. Therefore the Lord has kept the disaster in mind, and brought it upon us; for the Lord our God *is* righteous in all the works which He does, though we have not obeyed His voice. And now, O Lord our God, who brought Your people out of the land of Egypt with a mighty hand, and made Yourself a name, as *it is* this day—we have sinned, we have done wickedly! O Lord, according to all Your righteousness, I pray, let Your anger and Your fury be turned away from Your city Jerusalem, Your holy mountain; because for our sins, and for the iniquities of our fathers, Jerusalem and Your people *are* a reproach to all *those* around us. Now therefore, our God, hear the prayer of Your servant, and his supplications, and for the Lord's sake cause Your face to shine on Your sanctuary, which is desolate. O my God, incline Your ear and hear; open Your eyes and see our desolations, and the city which is called by Your name; for we do not present our supplications before You because of our righteous deeds, but because of Your great mercies. O Lord, hear! O Lord, forgive! O Lord, listen and act! Do not delay for Your own sake, my God, for Your city and Your people are called by Your name." (Dan. 9:1–19)

All that is left to say is "Amen!"

CHAPTER 14

THE FIRST AND SECOND DEATHS

I never knew for sure what happened to a person when he or she died until I studied the Bible. One would think there should be no confusion about this subject when the Bible is so clear about it. For this important subject, let us begin with John 11.

Lazarus, a close friend to Jesus, was sick. His two sisters sent a message to Jesus, saying, "Lord, behold, he whom you love is sick" (verse 3). Lazarus and his sisters, Martha and Mary, lived in Bethany, about fifteen-to-twenty miles from where Jesus was preaching beyond the Jordan. Instead of Jesus rushing to the side of His friend, He waited for two more days.

Apparently, the disciples, seeing Christ's delay, must have wondered why He had not gone to Bethany right away to cure His friend. Jesus must have sensed their feelings, so He said to them, "This sickness is not unto death, but for the glory of God, that the Son of God may be glorified through it" (verse 4). After the two days, Jesus finally said, "Let us go to Judea again" (verse 7). He added, "Our friend Lazarus sleeps, but I go that I may wake him up. Then His disciples said, 'Lord, if he sleeps, he will get well'" (verses 11, 12).

Jesus saw the disciples had misunderstood Him. "Then Jesus said to them plainly, 'Lazarus is dead. And I am glad for your sakes that I was not there, that you may believe. Nevertheless let us go to him'" (verses 14, 15). There was an important lesson the disciples were about to learn, and we need to learn it as well. Please notice Jesus compared death to sleep. Except for a few individuals noted specifically in the Bible, those who have died are not in heaven enjoying holy bliss with the angels. They are simply sleeping and waiting for the resurrection at the second coming, when Jesus will awaken the dead. Have you never heard of that before? Then read on.

The Bible teaches there are two deaths and two resurrections. The first death is the one all would experience if they died before Jesus' second coming.

Notice how Jesus describes this great truth: "Do not marvel at this; for the hour is coming in which all who are in the graves will hear His voice and come forth—those who have done good, to the resurrection of life, and those who have done evil, to the resurrection of condemnation" (John 5:28, 29). Again, please notice, *all* the dead hear the voice of the Master from the grave, not from heaven. Furthermore, you should want to be in the first resurrection, not the second:

> And I saw thrones, and they sat on them, and judgment was committed to them. Then *I saw* the souls of those who had been beheaded for their witness to Jesus and for the word of God ... And they lived and reigned with Christ for a thousand years. But the rest of the dead did not live again until the thousand years were finished. This *is* the first resurrection. Blessed and holy *is* he who has part in the first resurrection. Over such the second death has no power, but they shall be priests of God and of Christ, and shall reign with Him a thousand years. (Rev. 20:4–6)

Now, back to Lazarus. When Jesus finally arrived in Bethany at the home of Lazarus and his two sisters, notice what Martha said to Him. In fact, let us eavesdrop into their whole conversation. Beloved, you may have read this passage many times before, but we should understand the implication of these words anew:

> Now Martha said to Jesus, "Lord, if You had been here, my brother would not have died. But even now I know that whatever You ask of God, God will give You." Jesus said to her, "Your brother will rise again." Martha said to Him, "I know that he will rise again in the resurrection at the last day." Jesus said to her, "I am the resurrection and the life. He who believes in Me, though he may die, he shall live. And whoever lives and believes in Me shall never die. Do you believe this?" She said to Him, "Yes, Lord, I believe that You are the Christ, the Son of God, who is to come into the world." (John 11:21–27)

Dear reader, do you believe, like Martha did, that Jesus is the resurrection and the life? That's the only way anyone can be resurrected after death. Let us read a little further. It gets better. Now Jesus is ready to do exactly what He said He would do four days earlier: awaken Lazarus.

Therefore, when Jesus saw her weeping, and the Jews who came with her weeping, He groaned in the spirit and was troubled. And He said, "Where have you laid him?" They said to Him, "Lord, come and see." Jesus wept ... Then Jesus, again groaning in Himself, came to the tomb. It was a cave, and a stone lay against it. Jesus said, "Take away the stone." Martha, the sister of him who was dead, said to Him, "Lord, by this time there is a stench, for he has been dead four days." Jesus said to her, "Did I not say to you that if you would believe you would see the glory of God?" Then they took away the stone from the place where the dead man was lying. And Jesus lifted up His eyes and said, "Father, I thank You that You have heard Me. And I know that You always hear Me, but because of the people who are standing by I said this, that they may believe that You sent Me." Now when He had said these things, He cried with a loud voice, "Lazarus, come forth!" And he who had died came out bound hand and foot with grave clothes, and his face was wrapped with a cloth. Jesus said to them, "Loose him, and let him go." (John 11:33–44)

Lazarus did not have any story to tell about spending four days in heaven before he was resurrected by Jesus. Frankly, I would not have been a "happy camper" if I had to return to this earth after spending four days in heaven!

Dear reader, I recommend you read John 11 in full. We do not receive immortality/eternal life when we die. Again, *all* have to wait for the first or second resurrection. Again, Jesus made this fact even clearer. "This is the will of the Father who sent Me, that of all He has given Me I should lose nothing, but should raise it up at the last day" (John 6:39). Had He said it once, that would have been sufficient, but this reality is repeated multiple times in the same chapter (see verses 40, 44, 54).

The Lord did not want any honest soul to miss this important teaching. No, the body does not go to the grave [Hebrew *sheol*; Greek *hades*] while the soul goes to heaven. When God created Adam, He used the dust of the ground and breathed into his nostrils the breath of life. "And man became a living soul" (Gen. 2:7; some modern versions say, "Man became a living being"). Please notice it is the combination of the dust of the ground and the breath of God—these two entities—that equal a living soul. The opposite occurs when one is dead. "Then the dust will return to the earth as it was, And the spirit [or breath] will return to God who gave it" (Eccles. 12:7).

Furthermore, the following verses will shed more light on what happens to a person when he or she dies. The wisest man who ever lived, Solomon, wrote,

"The dead know nothing ... Also their love, their hatred, and their envy have now perished ... Whatever your hand finds to do, do it with your might; for there is no work or devise or knowledge or wisdom in the grave where you are going" (9:5, 6, 10). Bible heroes such as Job, David, Jeremiah, and Daniel, to name a few, all called death a "sleep" as they waited for the resurrection (see Job 14:10–12; Ps. 13:3; 146:4; Jer. 51:39, 57; Dan. 12:2).

Just as the Bible speaks about what happens to a person at death, it also speaks of a future judgment. We are not immediately taken to heaven or sentenced to hell when we die. Imagine, after spending 1,000 years or more in either heaven or hell, hearing God say, "Now it is time to receive your reward or punishment." John made it very clear that judgment precedes sentencing: "He who is unjust, let him be unjust still; he who is filthy, let him be filthy still; he who is righteous, let him be righteous still; he who is holy, let him be holy still. And behold, I am coming quickly, and My reward *is* with Me, to give to everyone according to his work" (Rev. 22:11, 12).

Reader, did you notice how these words agree with what Jesus said? "And this is the will of Him who sent Me, that everyone who sees the Son and believes in Him may have everlasting life; and I will raise him up *at the last day*" (John 6:40, emphasis added).

Paul corroborated this same truth when he wrote to his young "son in the faith": "Finally, there is laid up for me the crown of righteousness, which the Lord, the righteous Judge, will give to me on that Day, and not to me only but also to all who have loved His appearing" (2 Tim. 4:8). He shared this teaching with other believers as well:

> Behold, I tell you a mystery: We shall not all *sleep*, but we shall all be changed— in a moment, in the twinkling of an eye, at the *last trumpet*. For the trumpet will sound, and the dead will be raised incorruptible, and we shall be changed. For this corruptible must put on incorruption, and this mortal *must* put on immortality. So when this corruptible has put on incorruption, and this mortal has put on immortality, then shall be brought to pass the saying that is written: "Death is swallowed up in victory." (1 Cor. 15:51–55, emphasis added)
>
> For the Lord Himself will descend from heaven with a shout, with the voice of an archangel, and with the trumpet of God. And the dead in Christ will rise first. Then we who are alive *and* remain shall be caught up together with them in the clouds to meet the Lord in the air. And thus we shall

always be with the Lord. Therefore comfort one another with these words. (1 Thess. 4:16–18)

The sadness we experience when a loved one dies is beyond words. It is not hard to understand why many of us would prefer to believe he or she is in heaven; that can be very comforting … or is it? Can you imagine being in heaven immediately after death and witnessing a loved one's suffering? You would not be happy or enjoying holy bliss if a child, spouse, another family member, or dear friend was suffering excruciating pain on earth. Did you read with understanding the assurance in the above text? In the resurrection, Jesus will raise the dead first. Then those who are alive and remain shall be caught up together—yes, *together*—to meet the Lord in the air. "Therefore comfort one another with these words."

Beloved, be comforted with the truth of God's Word. If you believe and accept it, you will see your dead loved ones again. Let us, by God's grace and mercy, be faithful until the end.

With that said, what happens to those who "go to hell," you may be wondering? Let me make something very clear: While the Bible mentions the word "hell" many times, it does not teach that people who do not go to heaven spend eternity in hell. You have to read ancient historical books written by Plato and other philosophers to find where this dogma originated. While millions—indeed, billions—teach this brutal doctrine, it did not originate in the Bible. Yes, I was also shocked and pleasantly surprised to discover what the Bible says about the wicked dead. Please fasten your "mental seatbelt." Let us examine what Scripture teaches about this most important doctrine.

One of the most well-known verses in the entire Bible is John 3:16. How many times have you read this verse? Did you just read and memorize it or did you study and really understand it? Let us learn anew, with the help of the Holy Spirit, what this text teaches: "For God so loved the world that He gave His only begotten Son, that whoever believes in Him should not perish but have everlasting life." Additionally, "For God did not send His Son into the world to condemn the world, but that the world through Him might be saved" (verse 17). You may want to read these wonderful, comforting verses again before we proceed for our analysis.

Did you notice the opposite of "everlasting life" is "perish," not "eternal hell or damnation"? Yes, after the final judgment by God and His Son, there will be a reckoning for those who refuse to accept the blood of Jesus as their only salvation. However, it is called "death" or "the second death." Read these texts from the last book of the Bible:

> He that hath an ear, let him hear what the Spirit saith unto the churches; He that overcometh shall not be hurt of *the second death*. (Rev. 2:11, KJV, emphasis added)
>
> Blessed and holy is he that hath part in the first resurrection: on such *the second death* hath no power, but they shall be priests of God and of Christ, and shall reign with him a thousand years. (Rev. 20:6, KJV, emphasis added)
>
> And death and hell were cast into the lake of fire. This is *the second death*. (Rev. 20:14, KJV, emphasis added)
>
> But the fearful, and unbelieving, and the abominable, and murderers, and whoremongers, and sorcerers, and idolaters, and all liars, shall have their part in the lake which burneth with fire and brimstone: which is *the second death*. (Rev. 21:8, KJV, emphasis added)

You see, "the wages of sin is *death*; but the gift of God is *eternal life* through Jesus Christ our Lord" (Rom. 6:23, emphasis added). We have only two options: death or eternal life. There is no "purgatory" or "limbo." These are the inventions of the devil to attack and desecrate the reputation of our loving, merciful heavenly Father. It gets better (or worse), depending on the choice one makes regarding the glorious gift of Jesus' blood to rescue the sinner from the grip of the enemy.

> **We have only two options: death or eternal life. There is no "purgatory" or "limbo." These are the inventions of the devil to attack and desecrate the reputation of our loving, merciful heavenly Father.**

At this juncture, you may have some other relevant questions about Bible passages that seem to contradict the above ones. That's a fair sentiment. Let us study, not just read, some of those passages.

First of all, even if you can speak Hebrew or Greek, there are some linguistic principles you need to understand about the Bible. As I mentioned before, the book you are now reading is written for ordinary folks. I am not a scholar. Everything I am writing, I learned through prayerfully studying the Bible. I deeply believe it is the Holy Spirit who has been teaching me these wonderful truths. In fact, these truths are revolutionary for most people yet have been in the Bible for millennia.

The First and Second Deaths 79

In other words, what I am sharing has been known for ages by millions who have diligently studied the Bible with a humble spirit and attitude. I beg you, however, to carefully examine these truths for yourself and see what conclusion you glean from them. I am confident you will come up with the same conclusion millions of other sincere Bible students have throughout the ages.

I have a few more words on this subject and the language of the Bible before I conclude this chapter. While the Bible is a work of literature that has been translated into different languages, it is first and foremost inspired by the Holy Spirit, as I noted earlier. The Bible uses different literary tools to convey the truths of God to human beings in different languages: parables (see Matt. 13:34, 35); metaphors or figures of speech (see 19:23–26; Mark 10:24–27); idioms or allegories (see Gal. 4:22–24); poetry (see Psalms and Proverbs); symbolism (see 1 Cor. 11:23–26); and even powerful, exaggerated imagery.

To start, "He who loves father or mother more than Me is not worthy of Me. And he who loves son or daughter more than Me is not worthy of Me. And he who does not take his cross and follow after Me is not worthy of Me. He who finds his life will lose it, and he who loses his life for My sake will find it" (Matt. 10:37–39).

Compare that with Luke 14:26–27: "If anyone comes to Me and does not hate his father and mother, wife and children, brothers and sisters, yes, and his own life also, he cannot be My disciple. And whoever does not bear his cross and come after Me cannot be My disciple."

In reading the passage from Matthew, it sounds mild enough, but Luke used stronger images that, without understanding the context and biblical language, might cause some to come to a wrong understanding or conclusion. Please see another example on language:

> If your hand causes you to sin, cut it off. It is better for you to enter into life maimed, rather than having two hands, to go to hell, into the fire that shall never be quenched— where "Their worm does not die And the fire is not quenched." And if your foot causes you to sin, cut it off. It is better for you to enter life lame, rather than having two feet, to be cast into hell, into the fire that shall never be quenched— where "Their worm does not die And the fire is not quenched." And if your eye causes you to sin, pluck it out. It is better for you to enter the kingdom of God with one eye, rather than having two eyes, to be cast into hell fire— where "Their worm does not die And the fire is not quenched." For everyone will be seasoned with

fire, and every sacrifice will be seasoned with salt. Salt *is* good, but if the salt loses its flavor, how will you season it? Have salt in yourselves, and have peace with one another. (Mark 9:43–50)

Many are mystified by the Bible. One should not be surprised by this fact, however, because it declares itself to be coming from God. We must allow the Bible to interpret itself. Just as all languages have their own grammatical rules, the Bible has its own rules. Furthermore, since it is a book inspired by the Holy Spirit, in order to really know and understand it, one must be converted by the Spirit. The Bible calls it being "born again … of water and the Spirit" (John 3:3, 5; see chapter 3 of this book, "The Nicodemus Syndrome").

Paul succinctly put it this way: "But the natural man does not receive the things of the Spirit of God, for they are foolishness to him; nor can he know *them*, because they are spiritually discerned" (1 Cor. 2:14, NKJV). Let's read this text from a different modern translation: "But people who aren't spiritual can't receive these truths from God's Spirit. It all sounds foolish to them and they can't understand it, for only those who are spiritual can understand what the Spirit means" (NLT).

Hence, we must allow the author and interpreter of the Bible, the Holy Spirit, to teach us; and we should not attempt to conjure up our own private interpretation. The confusion of doctrines and so many denominations in this world is evidence of neglecting the following reality:

And so we have the prophetic word confirmed, which you do well to heed as a light that shines in a dark place, until the day dawns and the morning star rises in our hearts; knowing this first, that no prophecy of Scripture is of any private interpretation, for prophecy never came by the will of man, but holy men of God spoke *as they were* moved by the Holy Spirit. (2 Peter 1:19–21).

A good principle for Bible study that will significantly help is to study it by starting with clear, simple passages. That will assist the Bible student in understanding the more difficult passages. Do not start with idioms or metaphors that are more difficult to understand, especially when linguistic translation or understanding is at stake. Again, since most of us do not speak the original languages of the Bible, we must allow God to interpret it for us.

The apostle Peter, referring to Paul's writings, warned believers about destructive, harmful Bible reading:

> And consider *that* the longsuffering of our Lord *is* salvation—as also our beloved brother Paul, according to the wisdom given to him, has written to you, as also in all his epistles, speaking in them of these things, in which are some things hard to understand, which untaught and unstable *people* twist to their own destruction, as *they do* also the rest of the Scriptures. You therefore, beloved, since you know *this* beforehand, beware lest you also fall from your own steadfastness, being led away with the error of the wicked; but grow in the grace and knowledge of our Lord and Savior Jesus Christ. To Him *be* the glory both now and forever. Amen. (2 Peter 3:15-18)

With these facts in mind, let us conclude with what really happens to the dead who are not resurrected or translated to heaven during Christ's second coming. Please read the following passage again if you have missed this teaching about the final fate of the wicked:

> "For behold, the day is coming, Burning like an oven, And all the proud, yes, all who do wickedly will be stubble. And the day which is coming shall *burn them up*," Says the LORD of hosts, "That will leave them neither root nor branch. But to you who fear My name The Sun of Righteousness shall arise With healing in His wings; And you shall go out And grow fat like stall-fed calves. You shall trample the wicked, For they shall be *ashes* under the soles of your feet On the day that I do *this*," Says the LORD of hosts. (Mal. 4:1-3)

Beloved, this passage is very clear. Do you grasp the meaning of it and agree? Both the Old and the New Testaments teach that the wicked will perish—be burned to ashes—after the final judgment. Did you catch the word "ashes" in the text? Friends, ashes do not burn forever. To be sure, those who have spurned the love and saving mercy of God will be burned by "hell fire." However, when the just, righteous punishment has been completed, the impenitent will turn into ashes. It is against God's nature and character to eternally punish sinners who choose to be His enemies. Please listen from the depth of your soul while you read these words:

For when we were still without strength, in due time Christ died for the ungodly. For scarcely for a righteous man will one die; yet perhaps for a good man someone would even dare to die. But God demonstrates His own love toward us, in that while we were still sinners, Christ died for us. Much more then, having now been justified by His blood, we shall be saved from wrath through Him. For if when we were enemies we were reconciled to God through the death of His Son, much more, having been reconciled, we shall be saved by His life. And not only that, but we also rejoice in God through our Lord Jesus Christ, through whom we have now received the reconciliation. (Rom. 5:6–11)

Yes, evil, like a cancer, will be destroyed—burned up. Sin must be eradicated from the universe. And when it is destroyed, it will not exist anywhere in God's universe of love anymore. Sin will never raise its ugly head again. A prophet put it succinctly: "What do you conspire against the Lord? He will make an utter end of it. Affliction will not rise up a second time" (Nahum 1:9).

Just as Sodom and Gomorrah have never risen up again after they suffered the vengeance of eternal fire, neither will wickedness arise again in God's heaven or newly made earth. "As Sodom and Gomorrah, and the cities around them in a similar manner to these, having given themselves over to sexual immorality and gone after strange flesh, are set forth as an example, suffering the vengeance of eternal fire" (Jude 7).

Yes, Sodom and Gomorrah are the example of what will happen to the wicked in the last day. Friends, it is called "eternal fire" because the punishment is permanent. The separation from God will be forever. Once wickedness and evil have been extinguished, the universe will be cleansed, and God will make the earth new again. Those evil cities that existed so long ago are not still burning today. Praise the Lord for His righteous justice, grace, and mercy!

CHAPTER 15

WHAT DOES THE BIBLE MEAN BY "SOUL" AND "FOREVER"?

Learning to understand the Bible on its own terms is so fascinating. In other words, instead of coming to Scripture with our own private interpretations or some preconceived ideas, we must humble ourselves and sit at the feet of Jesus through the power of the Holy Spirit for instruction. Thus far, we have learned the Bible is inspired by God. We have also learned it interprets itself. One of the most pervasive characteristics of Satan is to "highjack" language to try to confuse people, especially those who are sincere, potential followers of God.

Take, for example, the English word "forever." It is not uncommon for English speakers to say "forever," knowing full well the duration is not long-lasting. Young people who "fall in love" will not hesitate to tell their partner, "I love you forever," yet that only lasts until another "love" interest comes along.

A common greeting for royalty in the Bible is the phrase, "O, king live forever" (see Neh. 2:3; Dan. 2:4; 3:9; 6:21). Even King Belshazzar, who saw "the fingers on the wall" and was about to be slain by the forces of Darius the Mede, was greeted in this respectful manner by the queen (perhaps his mother or grandmother—see 5:10-30). It was ironic because the acts that precipitated the untimely demise of the king could hardly segue him to eternal life, unless he were to confess and repent of his sins. Belshazzar had desecrated the sacred vessels of the God who held his breath in His hand and owned all his ways. Belshazzar had not glorified the God of heaven (see verse 23).

This brings me to another man: a reluctant prophet. According to Jonah, he spent "forever" in the belly of a big fish (see 2:6). Every young person who ever attended Sabbath or Sunday School knows Jonah "only" spent three days in the belly of the big fish. However, in retrospect, if I had spent three days inside a fish, no matter how large and cozy it was, that would seem to me to be forever.

Again, every language has its own idioms. Even the languages in which the Bible was written and translated are no different. One of the most moving Bible stories is that of Hannah, the wife of Elkanah. She lived at a time in Israel when, for a woman to be barren, was the most heart-rending, depressing experience. One can be sure Hannah's competition, the other wife, did not fail to make her life even more miserable. This was the situation in which Hannah found herself. After a long prayer vigil, with tears and supplication to God, the Lord granted her petition. A short time later, she conceived and bore a handsome baby boy and named him Samuel.

The astonishing thing is she then waited for what must have seemed to be such a short amount of time to her. That's when she brought her young son from the hill country of Ephraim to serve in the temple at Shiloh (about 1,000 miles away) "forever" (1 Sam. 1:22). This was in fulfillment of the vow made to God when she was praying for the boy. Soon, however, the text explains that Samuel was to serve the Lord "all the days of his life" or "as long as he lives" (verses 11, 28). Here we have it, friends. In the Bible, "forever" means "as long as a person lives" or "as long as a thing lasts."

Well, I can sense a question is coming: "Does that mean every time we read the word 'forever' in the Bible, it only means 'as long as one lives'?" No, not *every* time. A good rule to use is whether the subject of the sentence is God or a human being. The Bible states God is immortal and humans are mortal:

> That you keep [this] commandment without spot, blameless until our Lord Jesus Christ's appearing, which He will manifest in His own time, [He who is] the blessed and only Potentate, the King of kings and Lord of lords, *who alone has immortality*, dwelling in unapproachable light, whom no man has seen or can see, to whom [be] honor and everlasting power. Amen. (1 Tim. 6:14–16)

Did you read and understand this powerful truth about our Creator God? According to the Bible, not false prophets who teach otherwise, only the Creator God is immortal. This powerful, undeniable conclusion cannot and should not be bypassed casually. This is why every human being needs to go to God through Jesus Christ for the gift of eternal life. I hope, my friend, you will finally understand what Paul really meant when he said, "For the wages of sin *is* death, but the gift of God *is* eternal life in Christ Jesus our Lord" (Rom. 6:23).

The beloved apostle put it another way: "He who has the Son has life; he who does not have the Son of God does not have life. These things I have written to you who believe in the name of the Son of God, that you may know that you have eternal life, and that you may *continue to* believe in the name of the Son of God" (1 John 5:12, 13).

Beloved, please do not ever forget that eternal life is a gift to converted mortals, which God will give to sinners saved by grace. "For this corruptible must put on incorruption, and this mortal *must* put on immortality. So when this corruptible has put on incorruption, and this mortal has put on immortality, then shall be brought to pass the saying that is written: 'Death is swallowed up in victory'" (1 Cor. 15:53, 54).

Of course, this will occur when the faithful see Jesus at the resurrection—at His second coming. Read and listen to what Christ Himself said to a crowd that was following Him: "This is the will of the Father who sent Me, that of all He has given Me I should lose nothing, *but should raise it up at the last day*. And this is the will of Him who sent Me, that everyone who sees the Son and believes in Him may have everlasting life; *and I will raise him up at the last day*" (John 6:39, 40, emphasis added). If that is not sufficient, He used the phrase two other times (see verses 44, 54).

This is not a manmade teaching. It is a Bible teaching! Do you remember what God did after Adam and Eve sinned? "So He drove out the man; and He placed cherubim at the east of the garden of Eden, and a flaming sword which turned every way, to guard the way to the tree of life" (Gen. 3:24). Otherwise, Adam and Eve would have lived in sin eternally. The tree of life is "guarded" and reserved for obedient disciples of our Lord and Savior, Jesus Christ, in the earth made new.

Now, if immortality will be given to the saints at Christ's second coming, what will happen to the wicked who are not saved? That is a very good question. To put it simply, they will perish. "For God so loved the world that He gave His only begotten Son, that whoever believes in Him should not perish but have everlasting life" (John 3:16). "For the wages of sin *is* death, but the gift of God *is* eternal life in Christ Jesus our Lord" (Rom. 6:23). You see, friend, the result of sin is not eternal life in hell; it is death—the second death.

Jesus' parable of the sheep and the goats refers to the final separation of the righteous (sheep) and the wicked (goats). "And [the goats] will go away into everlasting punishment, but the righteous into eternal life" (Matt. 25:46). Remember, it is "everlasting punishment," not "everlasting punishing." Many teach that God will punish for eternity those who do not follow Him. Is it any wonder so many millions of people reject a "god" who could be so cruel and vindictive?

Yes, as mentioned before, the Bible teaches that the "tumor" of sin will be eradicated, not only from the earth, but from God's entire universe. Imagine again with me a loved one supposedly enjoying holy bliss in heaven while your mother, spouse, child, or best friend is endlessly suffering in the fire of hell somewhere in God's blessed, peaceful universe. What a mockery and blemish on the character of our loving, magnanimous God this would be!

> Imagine again with me a loved one supposedly enjoying holy bliss in heaven while your mother, spouse, child, or best friend is endlessly suffering in the fire of hell somewhere in God's blessed, peaceful universe. What a mockery and blemish on the character of our loving, magnanimous God this would be!

Again, let me remind you that the Bible teaches that the wicked—those who have shunned God's loving, unrelenting entreaty to be saved by the blood of Jesus—will be burned up—yes, with fire. The Bible actually calls it "eternal fire" or "everlasting fire."

Here is where millions—nay, billions—have been misled by the devil in using a phrase of the Bible out of context. By hijacking the language of Scripture, Satan has deceived men and women into believing God is bloodthirsty, barbaric, and merciless. In other words, he has tried (and apparently, in many cases, succeeded) for centuries to transfer his own characteristics onto our just, fair, loving Creator. The enemy has demonstrated his own character by the way he treated the Son of God, our Lord and Savior, Jesus Christ, while He was on earth. Satan continues to inspire wicked humans—his followers—to treat God's creation in a malicious way.

What about our souls? Aren't our souls immortal? God "*alone has immortality*, dwelling in unapproachable light, whom no man has seen or can see, to whom [be] honor and everlasting power. Amen" (1 Tim. 6:16, 17, emphasis added).

Well, that should satisfy the most honest seekers of Bible truth. However, for those who have been immersed in this false doctrine for a long time, please keep reading. "And the Lord God formed man *of* the dust of the ground, and breathed into his nostrils the breath of life; and man became a living soul" (Gen. 2:7 KJV; NKJV—"man became a living being").

Notice the text did not say God *gave* Adam a living soul; it says, "man *became* a living soul." Do you see the difference? Please take a deep breath and read the verse again, especially if this is the first time you've realized what a living soul is. I had to read it a few times myself the first time the Holy Spirit touched my mind about this subject. I am not making this up. Also, keep in mind that "the dust will return to the earth as it was, and the spirit will return to God who gave it" (Eccles. 12:7).

Now, let's do some math. It is the dust of the ground plus the breath of God that equals a living soul. When a person dies, the breath is separated from the dust, and that person is dead until Jesus returns and puts him or her all together again. By the way, that's why Paul called the resurrection "the blessed hope" (Titus 2:13).

Reader, I wish I was a Bible scholar so I could explain this better. Let me just leave you with two more passages on this subject. Please memorize them. "As Sodom and Gomorrah, and the cities around them in a similar manner to these, having given themselves over to sexual immorality and gone after strange flesh, are set forth as an example, suffering the vengeance of eternal fire" (Jude 7).

Did you get that? What happened to Sodom and Gomorrah is the "example" for those who will suffer "eternal fire" in the day of God's final judgment. The fire of Sodom and Gomorrah is not still burning now, after all of these millennia. The people did not have souls that are still burning. The *effect* is definitely eternal.

> "For behold, the day is coming, Burning like an oven, And all the proud, yes, all who do wickedly will be stubble. And the day which is coming shall burn them up," Says the LORD of hosts, "That will leave them neither root nor branch. But to you who fear My name, The Sun of Righteousness shall arise With healing in His wings; And you shall go out And grow fat like stall-fed calves. You shall trample the wicked, For they shall be ashes under the soles of your feet On the day that I do *this*," Says the LORD of hosts. (Mal. 4:1–3)

You see, the Hebrew and Greek words "sheol" and "hades," respectively, depict the common grave for both the righteous and the wicked. It is not a place of consciousness, as millions assume. This is why David wrote, "For You will not leave my soul in Sheol [hell], Nor will You allow Your Holy One to see corruption" (Ps. 16:10, NKJV). For your information, this verse was quoted by

Peter in the New Testament. Speaking about the death, burial, and resurrection of Jesus Christ, Peter used the prophesy of David to show that Christ was not left in the grave:

> Men of Israel, hear these words: Jesus of Nazareth, a Man attested by God to you by miracles, wonders, and signs which God did through Him in your midst, as you yourselves also know— Him, being delivered by the determined purpose and foreknowledge of God, you have taken by lawless hands, have crucified, and put to death; whom God raised up, having loosed the pains of death, because it was not possible that He should be held by it. For David says concerning Him: "I foresaw the LORD always before my face, For He is at my right hand, that I may not be shaken. Therefore my heart rejoiced, and my tongue was glad; Moreover my flesh also will rest in hope. For You will not leave my soul in Hades, Nor will You allow Your Holy One to see corruption." (Acts 2:22–27)

Let us allow Jesus to have the final words on this subject. "And do not fear those who kill the body but cannot kill the soul. But rather fear Him who is able to destroy both soul and body in hell" (Matt. 10:28).

Beloved, there you have it! I trust you have learned the other part of this concept, discussed in the previous chapter of this book.

CHAPTER 16

LIVING IN THE SHADOW OF THE JUDGMENT HOUR: THE STORY OF SODOM AND GOMORRAH

I think we could benefit if I write a few words about judgment. In my first few years of driving, I must have averaged at least one automobile accident a month, not to mention many moving and parking violations. In time, however, I came to consider myself an "excellent" driver. I further affirmed this self-assurance by not being involved in an accident or getting a summons for about fifteen years. However, not too long ago, I found myself having to answer three summonses in front of a traffic court judge in less than a year.

Boy, did I pray before each court appearance! My prayers were answered. Three times in the last year or so, I was able to come out of the courtroom with favorable decisions. Prayer works, especially when it is earnestly, sincerely practiced before a crisis.

There is a day of judgment coming that is much more serious than a few summonses in traffic court are. *Now* is the time for us to have a relationship with and pray to God before it is too late. Living in this dangerous world, we cannot wait any longer. We must send our petitions to and pray for His guidance now.

Some things are hard to understand. It is a good idea to pray about and study these issues earnestly in order to understand them. In the Bible, the Lord informs us of the Judgment Day through illustrations, object lessons, and other examples. We should not wait for that judgment to arrive but get ready for it today. We are to make sure we are right with God *now*. What happened in Sodom and Gomorrah could happen to us. There are lessons from those cities that are especially relevant for people living on the verge of a larger-scale devastation just ahead.

The Bible shows a great paradox. The way people choose to live and behave affects their future since they are living in the shadow of a calamitous event. This was the case in the Bible for a man named Lot, who lived in Sodom. Angels went to his house to warn him of the impending doom about to happen to that wicked city. However, Lot's family saw no urgency to get out. Little did Lot and his sons-in-law know that while they were continuing with business as usual, going with the flow and having a good time in Sodom, the most severe judgment was about to fall upon their city and its surrounding areas. Lot made a weak attempt to gather his family, but most of the family members just laughed at him.

To give us a better understanding of this family's behavior, let us read the story:

> Lot then went out and told his sons-in-law (they had married his daughters), "Get out of here! The LORD is going to destroy this city!" But his sons-in-law thought he was joking.
>
> As dawn was breaking, the angels pressured Lot. "Get going!" they told him. "Take your wife and your two daughters who are here, or you will be engulfed by the devastation that's coming to this city." But Lot kept lingering in the city, so the men grabbed his hand and the hands of his wife and two daughters (because of the LORD's compassion for him!), brought them out of the city, and left them outside. Then one of [the angels] said, "Flee for your lives! Don't look back or stop anywhere on the plain. Escape to the hills, or you'll be swept away!" "No! Please, my lords!" Lot pleaded with them. "Your servant has found favor in your sight, and you have shown me your gracious love in how you have dealt with me by keeping me alive. I cannot escape to the hills, because I'm afraid the disaster will overtake me, and I'll die. Look, there is a town nearby where I can flee, and it's a small one. Let me escape there! It's a small one, isn't it? That way I'll stay alive!" "All right," the angel replied to Lot, "I'll agree with your request! I won't overthrow the town that you mentioned. Hurry up and flee there, because I cannot do anything until you get to that town." Therefore the name of the town was called Zoar. (Gen. 19:14–22)

This "small" city was also marked to be destroyed. Zoar was no different from Sodom or the other cities. Soon afterward, Lot had to flee from there also. "Then Lot went up out of Zoar and dwelt in the mountains, and his two daughters were with him; for he was afraid to dwell in Zoar. And he and his two daughters dwelt in a cave" (verse 30).

You see, dear reader, long residence in Sodom had made Lot lukewarm and dull of hearing the warnings of God. In a real sense, he was getting tired of living the Christian life. He was becoming weary of well-doing and in danger of slipping toward a kind of religious formalism. Lot's wife was even more affected. She disobeyed the commands God had sent through the angels and looked back to watch Sodom burn. She turned into a pillar of salt (see verse 26). Jesus warned us to "Remember Lot's wife" (Luke 17:32).

Many of the churches today are not that different. The Bible tells us to get out of "Babylon" and not turn back. In case we are tempted to judge Lot, his wife, or his sons-in-laws too harshly, we should take heed so as not to condemn ourselves in the process. Paul warned faultfinders this way:

> Therefore you are inexcusable, O man, whoever you are who judge, for in whatever you judge another you condemn yourself; for you who judge practice the same things. But we know that the judgment of God is according to truth against those who practice such things. And do you think this, O man, you who judge those practicing such things, and doing the same, that you will escape the judgment of God? Or do you despise the riches of His goodness, forbearance, and longsuffering, not knowing that the goodness of God leads you to repentance? But in accordance with your hardness and your impenitent heart you are treasuring up for yourself wrath in the day of wrath and revelation of the righteous judgment of God, who 'will render to each one according to his deeds:' eternal life to those who by patient continuance in doing good seek for glory, honor, and immortality; but to those who are self-seeking and do not obey the truth, but obey unrighteousness—indignation and wrath, tribulation and anguish, on every soul of man who does evil, of the Jew first and also of the Greek; but glory, honor, and peace to everyone who works what is good, to the Jew first and also to the Greek. For there is no partiality with God. (Rom. 2:1–11)

Jesus issued a similar warning: "Likewise as it was also in the days of Lot: They ate, they drank, they bought, they sold, they planted, they built; but on the day that Lot went out of Sodom it rained fire and brimstone from heaven and destroyed *them* all. Even so will it be in the day when the Son of Man is revealed" (Luke 17:28–30). We should not be satisfied or comfortable with living in Sodom, singing Sodom's songs, or dancing to the beat of Sodom's music. By doing that, we can become indifferent to spiritual things.

This brings us to our own modern Sodom: Babylon.

CHAPTER 17

THE WINE OF BABYLON

Now we are ready to study a bit more about Babylon. The word "Babylon" is derived from the incident that happened at the Tower of Babel. When the inhabitants of the ancient world, after the flood, tried to build a high tower to escape another flood, the Lord came down and confused their language in order to stop them from forming a confederacy of evil. Hence, the word "Babylon" started from the city Babel.

In the context of the book of Revelation, the author, John, used the word "Babylon" to mean confusion—the ability to confuse. The church called "Babylon" has taken actions and made statements that are inconsistent with the Word of God yet maintains that it is affirming the truth. For example, if a church teaches, among other things, that when a person dies, he or she goes immediately to heaven or hell, that would be inconsistent with the Word of God because at the same time, that church also teaches that there will be a future judgment when Christ returns.

In other words, one is sentenced to hell now yet will also be judged in the future. This and other spurious doctrines are very confusing to people on the earth. The "wine of Babylon" is symbolic of the confusion of the beliefs or philosophies the enemy of God brewed up to make the world drink of those errors. Babylon permeates and fits into whatever lifestyle or character is needed to do its diabolical schemes.

The wine of Babylon, therefore, is a system of doctrines that causes or is structured in a way to make people act inebriated. "Those who linger long at the wine … At the last it bites like a serpent, And stings like a viper. And your heart will utter perverse things" (Prov. 23:30–33). This religious system of beliefs provides the means to rationalize and make excuses for one's own sins and whatever we want to achieve on our own.

You recall, in the story of Lot and his family, the angels had to grab their hands to save them out of Sodom, which was about to be consumed with eternal fire, because "the Lord [is] merciful" (Gen. 19:16). Of course, Lot's wife did not make it to safety. Somehow, she was too attached to the family and the dainties left behind in Sodom. Jesus warned and reminded his disciples to "Remember Lot's wife" (Luke 17:32). This warning of Jesus is for those who will be living in the last days in a situation just like Sodom's.

You may ask, "How is the whole sophisticated world to be led to drink from this 'golden cup full of abomination'?" In other words, how is this "woman" so successful in leading (or deceiving) "the whole world" to drink from her doctrines and philosophies? It is because we are dealing with the most powerful rebel angel who fell from grace in heaven and is now inspiring Babylon. It these last days, we are not dealing with minor inconsistencies, trivial lies, or marginal errors. This is complete manipulation, using supreme, stealthy deceptions. This type of manipulation is so deep-rooted and ingrained in our being, it will take a major "surgery"; only a miracle of God could save us.

Scripture tells the story of Achan as part of the battles of Jericho and Ai:

> But the children of Israel committed a trespass regarding the accursed things, for Achan ... of the tribe of Judah, took of the accursed things ... So the Lord said to Joshua ... "Israel has sinned, and they have also transgressed My covenant which I commanded them. For they have even taken some of the accursed things, and have both stolen and deceived; and they have also put *it* among their own stuff." (Josh. 7:1, 10, 11)

We cannot be like Achan, who perished because he could not resist stealing a Babylonian garment during the Israelites' battle of Jericho, which resulted in Israel's defeat in Ai. We must be completely converted.

Babylon and the beast of Revelation are synonymous. Their powers derive from Satan. "The whole earth marveled as they followed the beast.... Also it causes all, both small and great, both rich and poor, both free and slave, to be marked on the right hand or the forehead, so that no one can buy or sell unless he has the mark, that is, the name of the beast or the number of its name" (Rev. 13:3, 16, 17, ESV). This is serious; yes, it is beyond serious. It is a matter of life and death—not just worldly death, but spiritual, eternal death! Those who drink the wine of Babylon will persecute God's true people.

John had more to say about this fallen woman:

Then one of the seven angels who had the seven bowls came and said to me, "Come, I will show you the judgment of the great prostitute who is seated on many waters, with whom the kings of the earth have committed sexual immorality, and with the wine of whose sexual immorality the dwellers on earth have become drunk." And he carried me away in the Spirit into a wilderness, and I saw a woman sitting on a scarlet beast that was full of blasphemous names, and it had seven heads and ten horns. The woman was arrayed in purple and scarlet, and adorned with gold and jewels and pearls, holding in her hand a golden cup full of abominations and the impurities of her sexual immorality. And on her forehead was written a name of mystery: Babylon the great, mother of prostitutes and of earth's abominations. And I saw the woman, drunk with the blood of the saints, the blood of the martyrs of Jesus. When I saw her, I marveled greatly. (Rev. 17:1–6, ESV)

When John saw that vision, he was astonished. The angel that was dispatched to give him this message gave him the meaning of the woman and the beast. This woman is the same woman John called "Babylon": "And another angel followed, saying, 'Babylon is fallen, is fallen, that great city, because she has made all nations drink of the wine of the wrath of her fornication'" (14:8, NKJV).

Now let us continue the explanation of the angel:

But the angel said to me, "Why did you marvel? I will tell you the mystery of the woman and of the beast that carries her, which has the seven heads and the ten horns. The beast that you saw was, and is not, and will ascend out of the bottomless pit and go to perdition. And those who dwell on the earth will marvel, whose names are not written in the Book of Life from the foundation of the world, when they see the beast that was, and is not, and yet is. Here *is* the mind which has wisdom: The seven heads are seven mountains on which the woman sits. There are also seven kings. Five have fallen, one is, *and* the other has not yet come. And when he comes, he must continue a short time. The beast that was, and is not, is himself also the eighth, and is of the seven, and is going to perdition. The ten horns which you saw are ten kings who have received no kingdom as yet, but they receive authority for one hour as kings with the beast. These are of one mind, and they will give their power and authority to the beast. These will make war with the Lamb, and the Lamb will overcome them, for He is Lord of lords and King of kings; and those *who are* with Him *are* called, chosen, and faithful.' Then he said to me, 'The waters which you saw, where the harlot sits, are peoples, multitudes, nations, and tongues." (Rev. 17:7–15, NKJV)

Before we go any further, let us note a few important codes from the angel's explanation: First, the woman is "the great prostitute who is seated on many waters." The waters represent peoples, multitudes, nations, and tongues/languages (verse 15). The seven heads and ten horns are kings or leaders (verses 10, 12). "These are of one mind and they will give their power and authority to the beast" (verse 13).

The Lord had sent these important, precise messages to warn His people about how the leaders of Babylon (Rome) have caused "all nations to drink of the wine of Babylon." Please note that John used the name "Babylon" to describe the Roman Empire. Today, we understand this message is not simply a warning about civil Rome but subsequently papal Rome. The Bible uses the pronoun "she," the feminine gender to depict a church.

There is a woman in Revelation that depicts the true church:

> Now a great sign appeared in heaven: a woman clothed with the sun, with the moon under her feet, and on her head a garland of twelve stars. Then being with child, she cried out in labor and in pain to give birth. And another sign appeared in heaven: behold, a great, fiery red dragon having seven heads and ten horns, and seven diadems on his heads. His tail drew a third of the stars of heaven and threw them to the earth. And the dragon stood before the woman who was ready to give birth, to devour her Child as soon as it was born. She bore a male Child who was to rule all nations with a rod of iron. And her Child was caught up to God and His throne. (Rev. 12:1–5)

The woman in Revelation 17 represents the false church. "I saw a woman [church] sit upon a scarlet-colored beast, full of names of blasphemy, having seven heads and ten horns. The woman was arrayed in purple and scarlet, and adorned with gold and precious stones and pearls, having in her hand a golden cup full of abominations and the filthiness of her fornication" (17:3, 4). This is a very rich church.

Furthermore, Babylon has practically deceived the whole world with its dogmas and false worship. John added, "Upon her forehead was a name written, MYSTERY, BABYLON THE GREAT, THE MOTHER OF HARLOTS AND

Abominations Of The Earth.... And the woman whom you saw is that great city which reigns over the kings of the earth" (verses 5, 18). She reigns over the civil leaders of this world.

A fourth angel amplifies this message by saying, "For all the nations have drunk of the wine of the wrath of her fornication, the kings of the earth have committed fornication with her, and the merchants of the earth have become rich through the abundance of her luxury" (18:3). Again, the question should be asked: How is the whole sophisticated world deceived and led to drink from this woman's "golden cup full of abominations"? In other words, how is this "woman" so successful in leading (or deceiving) "the whole world" to drink or receive her blasphemous doctrines? Before we go forward, there is another question that needs to be answered: What is the meaning of "full of names of blasphemy"?

Jesus was accused of blasphemy several times because He had said He was the Son of God. "Then the Jews took up stones again to stone Him. Jesus answered them, 'Many good works I have shown you from My Father. For which of those works do you stone Me?' The Jews answered Him, saying, 'For a good work we do not stone You, but for blasphemy, and because You, being a Man, make Yourself God'" (John 10:31–33).

Again, "the high priest tore his clothes, saying, 'He has spoken blasphemy! What further need do we have of witnesses? Look, now you have heard His blasphemy!'" (Matt. 26:65). Of course, Jesus did not commit blasphemy because He was indeed God in the flesh. However, when any mortal claims he or she is God on earth or takes prerogatives that only belong to Him, that person is guilty of blasphemy.

The "beast" is none other than a powerful religious church leader whom the whole world—leaders and common people alike—follow as the so-called representative of God on earth. He gets his power from the dragon. This is the same "great dragon" who was cast out of heaven, "that serpent of old, called the Devil and Satan, who deceives the whole world; he was cast to the earth, and his angels were cast out with him" (Rev. 12:9, NKJV).

> Then I stood on the sand of the sea. And I saw a beast rising up out of the sea, having seven heads and ten horns, and on his horns ten crowns, and on his heads a blasphemous name. Now the beast which I saw was like a leopard, his feet were like *the feet of* a bear, and his mouth like the mouth of a lion. The dragon gave him his power, his throne, and great authority. And I saw one of his heads as if it had been mortally wounded, and his deadly

wound was healed. And all the world marveled and followed the beast. So they worshiped the dragon who gave authority to the beast; and they worshiped the beast, saying, "Who *is* like the beast? Who is able to make war with him?" And he was given a mouth speaking great things and blasphemies, and he was given authority to continue for forty-two months. Then he opened his mouth in blasphemy against God, to blaspheme His name, His tabernacle, and those who dwell in heaven. (Rev. 13:1–6, NKJV)

Hence, the second angel's message in 14:8 says the rich church is making people of the earth "drink of the wine"—its false doctrines. Of course, in due time, she will be judged by God Himself. His wrath will fall on her for her rampant "fornication."

Therefore, our only safeguard against this dangerous, evil power is earnest prayer to God and the study of His Word in the power of the Holy Spirit for protection. Even Jesus needed to pray. "Now it came to pass in those days that He went out to the mountain to pray, and continued all night in prayer to God" (Luke 6:12). Reader, please do not miss this incredible verse. What a sobering, penetrating thought! The King of kings and Lord of lords needed time to pray—all night—to overcome evil forces. What about us? What about us sinful, spiritually frail humans?

> What a sobering, penetrating thought! The King of kings and Lord of lords needed time to pray—all night—to overcome evil forces. What about us? What about us sinful, spiritually frail humans?

I once asked a group of children, "Why do you think Jesus, the Son of God, needed to pray so fervently?"

One student answered, "Jesus needed power."

Another student stated, "Jesus needed wisdom."

A third answered, "Jesus needed strength to withstand temptations."

To summarize what these wise children understood, Jesus needed power, wisdom, and strength to overcome the dragon who gave the beast power, position, and great authority (see Rev. 13:2). Beloved, we need the same spiritual power the Savior of the world exercised to overcome this malignant force.

Paul shared this advice: "And do not be drunk with wine, in which is dissipation; but be filled with the Spirit, (Eph. 5:18, NKJV). May the Lord help us to avail ourselves of this power, wisdom, and strength, which He is willing to give to all of His children who ask.

CHAPTER 18

THE LAST MESSAGE FROM GOD

Beloved, something momentous is about to happen on this earth, and we have no idea about it. It will be something more devastating than what happened to Sodom and Gomorrah. Like the people of those doomed towns, many of us have become dull and apathetic spiritually. We are comfortable with our sinful lives. In our eyes, we are good people. We don't need anything else. We may feel we are better than religious folks are and doing all the right things, but inwardly, we are just cold and dry, with no spiritual power.

Some of us are just nominal Christians. We were born and raised in the church, and this is all we know. Sometimes, we go to church for Christmas and/or Easter, and that seems sufficient for us. Others came into the church at an early age, but there has been no difference in their lives since then. We know the practices and religious lingos very well. We are very comfortable in the church environment.

The Hebrew church, in the time of Christ, faced the same conditions in which we find ourselves. Persecution by the Roman Empire was about to break out, but the ancient people were oblivious to the approaching calamity that was soon to fall on them. Like the wicked people in Sodom, they were going through their everyday routines. Therefore, Paul sent this solemn admonition to help us:

> Let us draw near with a true heart in full assurance of faith, having our hearts sprinkled from an evil conscience and our bodies washed with pure water. Let us hold fast the confession of *our* hope without wavering, for He who promised *is* faithful. And let us consider one another in order to stir up love and good works, not forsaking the assembling of ourselves together, as *is* the manner of some, but exhorting *one another*, and so much the more as you see the Day approaching. (Heb. 10:22–25)

God will never send destruction upon the earth without giving people sufficient warning. You can be sure, as people living in these last days, God has given His prophets messages to warn us of His coming. Consider the following passage, known as "the three angels' messages":

> And I saw another angel fly in the midst of heaven, having the everlasting gospel to preach unto them that dwell on the earth, and to every nation, and kindred, and tongue, and people, Saying with a loud voice, Fear God, and give glory to him; for the hour of his judgment is come: and worship him that made heaven, and earth, and the sea, and the fountains of waters. And there followed another angel, saying, Babylon is fallen, is fallen, that great city, because she made all nations drink of the wine of the wrath of her fornication. And the third angel followed them, saying with a loud voice, If any man worship the beast and his image, and receive his mark in his forehead, or in his hand, The same shall drink of the wine of the wrath of God, which is poured out without mixture into the cup of his indignation; and he shall be tormented with fire and brimstone in the presence of the holy angels, and in the presence of the Lamb: And the smoke of their torment ascendeth up forever and ever: and they have no rest day nor night, who worship the beast and his image, and whoever receiveth the mark of his name. Here is the patience of the saints: here are they that keep the commandments of God, and the faith of Jesus. (Rev. 14:6–12, KJV)

This passage is referring to a very important message God has sent to this lost planet to warn us of important events just before Christ returns. Again, even though it is an old message, it is written for people who live in these last days of earth's history. It is so important and urgent that it is symbolized by three angels flying swiftly in the heavens to warn earth's inhabitants, "those who dwell on the earth—to every nation, tribe, tongue, and people" (verse 6, NKJV).

Let us understand something right from the beginning. It is very unlikely we will visibly see three angels flying in the sky preaching on this side of eternity. These three angels represent three messages God has commissioned His true followers on earth to preach to people in this world. If you have never heard or understood these messages before, you are about to hear and comprehend them today.

The First Angel's Message: John said, "Then I saw another angel flying in the midst of heaven, having the everlasting gospel to preach to those who dwell on the earth—to every nation, tribe, tongue, and people— saying with a loud voice, 'Fear God and give glory to Him, for the hour of His judgment has come; and worship Him who made heaven and earth, the sea and springs of water" (verses 6, 7).

The first, most important thing about this message is the preaching of "the everlasting gospel." The word "gospel" means "good news." I am sure you know the best news in the Bible is the fact that the Son of God came to this planet to die for our sins. After He resurrected, He ascended back to heaven.

> Moreover, brethren, I declare to you the gospel which I preached to you, which also you received and in which you stand, by which also you are saved, if you hold fast that word which I preached to you—unless you believed in vain. For I delivered to you first of all that which I also received: that Christ died for our sins according to the Scriptures, and that He was buried, and that He rose again the third day according to the Scriptures. (1 Cor. 15:1–4, NKJV)

To put it succinctly, the gospel is the death, burial, and the resurrection of Jesus Christ to ransom us from the grip of sin, death, and the devil. This is the message God wants to be preached to all the world before Jesus' second coming.

Yes, some may find it hard to believe that in a world with so many churches, preachers, satellites, the internet, and all the other electronic devices, there are people who have never heard about the good news of salvation. Perhaps, it is not that people have never heard about this message, but rather, for many, what is being preached today is not the everlasting gospel of Jesus Christ.

Essentially, we are talking about a loving God who wants to give everyone on earth a last chance to accept eternal life through His Son, Jesus Christ, who shed His precious blood on the cross of Calvary to save us sinners. Another reason why it is hard for many to hear this message is we have become "dull of hearing" the truth of God, written in the Bible. The worries of the world have occupied our minds, and we cannot hear.

Peter warned people not to be callous about God's promise to return a second time. "The Lord is not slow about His promise, as some count slowness, but is patient toward you, not wishing for any to perish but for all to come to repentance. But the day of the Lord will come like a thief, in which the heavens will pass away with a roar and the elements will be destroyed with intense heat, and the earth and its works will be burned up" (2 Peter 3:9–11, NASB).

Before that great inferno, Jesus Himself said, "And this gospel of the kingdom will be preached in all the world as a witness to all the nations, and then the end will come" (Matt. 24:14, NKJV).

The preaching of the everlasting gospel is just the beginning of the first angel's message. What else is this "angel" telling us? "Fear God and give glory to Him, for the hour of His judgment has come; and worship Him who made heaven and earth, the sea and springs of water." We give glory to God by respecting and obeying His commandments, which most of the world has nearly forgotten. That urgent message needs to be preached at this critical time.

It is evident that even though we have so many churches and preachers "preaching" about God, they are not preaching about the Creator God or this message. If they were, there would be no necessity for Him to send this urgent message to warn people to worship the One "who made heaven, and earth, and the sea." There would have been no point in emphasizing these messages if they already took root in people's hearts. If these messages were being preached all along, it would be pointless to call such urgent attention to them. Let us unravel these mysterious messages further and see if you have ever heard or understood them.

The Second Angel's Message: John continued, "And there followed another angel [a second one], saying, Babylon is fallen, is fallen, that great city, because she made all nations drink of the wine of the wrath of her fornication" (Rev. 14:8). When John wrote these words, the ancient kingdom of Babylon had been extinct since about 539 BC. John is referring to the superpower that was ruling in his days and beyond. You see, he was a prisoner of the Romans on the island of Patmos, near Greece.

The resurrected Savior gave John these solemn messages to send to the seven churches in Asia Minor and, by extension, to His people who would live in these last days. These messages are for people who would be affected by religious and political confusion and persecution. Obviously, they were coded to make sure they arrived intact to the believers. What about the part of the message that mentions Babylon had made "all nations drink of the wine of the wrath of her fornication"? We will study Revelation 17 more deeply in the next chapter to gain additional details to help us decode this solemn message about spiritual Babylon.

The Third Angel's Message: The third angel's message is no less ominous:

> And the third angel followed them, saying with a loud voice, If any man worship the beast and his image, and receive [his] mark in his forehead, or

in his hand, The same shall drink of the wine of the wrath of God, which is poured out without mixture into the cup of his indignation; and he shall be tormented with fire and brimstone in the presence of the holy angels, and in the presence of the Lamb: And the smoke of their torment ascendeth up forever and ever: and they have no rest day nor night, *who worship the beast and his image*, and whosoever receives the mark of his name. (Rev. 14:9–11, KJV, emphasis added)

Please understand that at this point, when the Bible mentions the seal of God or the mark of the beast, it is referring to whom we choose to worship in our foreheads (i.e., minds, frontal lobes of our brains), especially just prior to Christ's second coming. For now, please notice John is referring to worship.

Dear reader, as we go on, keep in mind it has always been about worship! Again, Babylon (the beast) is a religious entity moved by Satan (the dragon) to force the whole world to worship him instead of the Living God.

Let us further review this message. Although the words change from "Babylon" to "the beast and his image," the message does not change. The Bible is simply using different figures or symbols to describe the same message. A beast or horn in the Bible represents a civil government, religious power, or leader. That is to say, it can be a king, kingdom, nation, or powerful religious leader.

In Daniel, we also have that same description. An angel defined these symbols: "The fourth beast shall be the fourth kingdom upon earth, which shall be diverse from all kingdoms, and shall devour the whole earth, and shall tread it down, and break it in pieces" (7:23, KJV). Babylon and the beast are synonymous. The message is that we should not worship Babylon or receive the mark of the beast in our foreheads or hands.

Again, this mark of the beast in the forehead or hand is the opposite of the seal of God in the forehead. We have to allow the Lord to place His seal in our foreheads to confirm we worship Him rather than Satan or his hosts of imposters. It is either the seal of God or the mark of the beast. There is no other option.

Whom do we worship? That will be the issue for those who live in these last days of earth's history. Are we going to worship God or the beast and his

> **Whom do we worship? That will be the issue for those who live in these last days of earth's history. Are we going to worship God or the beast and his supporters? To know and follow the warnings of these messages is a matter of life and death!**

supporters? To know and follow the warnings of these messages is a matter of life and death!

These three messages conclude with the following statement: "Here is the patience of the saints: here are they that keep the commandments of God, and the faith of Jesus" (Rev. 14:12). We are to patiently wait as we worship God by keeping His commandments in spite of living in a world that worships a blasphemous usurper masquerading as God. And, as God's people, we are to hold to the faith of Jesus Christ, who saves us by His marvelous grace.

Moreover, the warnings of Revelation do not end here. A fourth angel was dispatched from heaven with additional admonitions:

> And after these things, I saw another angel [a fourth one], come down from heaven, having great power; and the earth was lightened with his glory. And he cried mightily with a strong voice, saying, Babylon the great is fallen, is fallen, and is become the habitation of devils, and the hold of every foul spirit, and a cage of every unclean and hateful bird. For all nations have drunk of the wine of the wrath of her fornication, and the kings of the earth have committed fornication with her, and the merchants of the earth are waxed rich through the abundance of her delicacies. And I heard another voice from heaven, saying, *Come out of her, my people, that ye be not partakers of her sins*, and that ye receive not of her plagues. For her sins have reached unto heaven, and God hath remembered her iniquities. Reward her even as she rewarded you, and double unto her double according to her works: in the cup which she hath filled fill to her double. (Rev. 18:1–6, emphasis added)

We cannot be saved while remaining in Babylon. We need Jesus, who alone can unmask the imposter and save us from his wrath. That's why the message is to "get out of Babylon." Long-term residence in Babylon has deadened the spiritual sensitivity of God's people. We get too comfortable living in Babylon. We invest so little capital in knowing God because we are busy investing in worldly markets. Getting out of Babylon is not an option; we either get out or perish, just like those who remained in Sodom.

This message is clear. Whatever, whomever, or wherever you are worshipping that is not consistent with all of God's Ten Commandments, you need to get out of it. This woman (i.e., church) is practicing fornication, which is breaking God's law. This is how the Bible describes the preparation of God's people, compared to those who follow the enemy and have rejected God prior to this great separation:

> And every man that hath this hope in him purifieth himself, even as he is pure. Whosoever committeth sin transgresseth also the law: for sin is the transgression of the law. And ye know that he was manifested to take away our sins; and in him is no sin. Whosoever abideth in him sinneth not: whosoever sinneth hath not seen him, neither known him. Little children, let no man deceive you: he that doeth righteousness is righteous, even as he is righteous. He that committeth sin is of the devil; for the devil sinneth from the beginning. For this purpose the Son of God was manifested, that he might destroy the works of the devil. Whosoever is born of God doth not commit sin; for his seed remaineth in him: and he cannot sin, because he is born of God. In this the children of God are manifest, and the children of the devil: whosoever doeth not righteousness is not of God, neither he that loveth not his brother. (1 John 3:3–10, KJV)

Did you understand this description? Sin is the transgression of God's law (verse 4). I know from firsthand experience it is not easy to separate from loved ones and friends to obey God, but the message from His Word cannot be clearer or more adamant about getting out of Babylon. "And I heard another voice from heaven, saying, Come out of her, my people, that ye be not partakers of her sins, and that ye receive not of her plagues" (Rev. 18:4).

God does not want His people to be partakers of her sins or receive of her plagues. A loving God is unwilling to let anyone perish, let alone His obedient children. "The Lord is not slack concerning His promise, as some count slackness, but is longsuffering toward us, not willing that any should perish but that all should come to repentance" (2 Peter 3:9, NKJV). Therefore, I write this book to share with my family, friends, and all others who are willing to learn what the Bible actually says, because I love you all!

Beloved, we need to examine ourselves to see if we are simple, nominal, or dedicated Christians. "Examine yourselves *as to* whether you are in the faith. Test yourselves. Do you not know yourselves, that Jesus Christ is in you?—unless indeed you are disqualified. But I trust that you will know that we are not disqualified" (2 Cor. 13:5, 6). It is such an examination that will help us to see if Christ's righteous living and obedience to His Father is being manifested in our lives. Living and having the attitude of Christ toward others (especially those who are different from us) is proof we are heading in the right direction. This is the honest examination of and the remedy of detoxification from our compromising ways with "the wine of Babylon" that are required of us.

We need to ask our merciful God for the fortitude and strength to get out of Babylon. He has promised, "And whatever we ask, we receive from Him, because we keep His commandments and do those things that are pleasing in His sight" (1 John 3:22). A bit earlier, John warned, "My little children, let us not love in word or in tongue, but in deed and in truth" (verse 18).

My friends, do not be fooled by those who are preaching "peace and safety" at this time. Just as in the days of Sodom and its surrounding cities, we, too, are living in the shadow of the judgment hour. Jesus urged us to "hold fast what you have till I come" (Rev. 2:25). When we hold fast, what we are holding is not a weak object that is ready to be broken. We are holding onto the mighty, powerful hands of God. This is not just a profession of faith but a commitment to the Lord of our salvation. This is where faith, works, and responsibility come together. We become more like Jesus. We do not just talk faith but live our lives in a solid commitment to God and our Savior, Jesus Christ.

> Therefore do not cast away your confidence, which has great reward. For you have need of endurance, so that after you have done the will of God, you may receive the promise: "For yet a little while, *And* He who is coming will come and will not tarry. Now the just shall live by faith; But if *anyone* draws back, My soul has no pleasure in him." But we are not of those who draw back to perdition, but of those who believe to the saving of the soul. (Heb. 10:35–39)

In this momentous time, many in the world are ignoring these solemn, important messages. Even professed Christians have no idea about what they mean. Furthermore, these messages are a clear warning to confirm the fact that we are living in the shadow of the final judgment hour. Perhaps you are wondering, 'How do I know it is the last message of warning for the people living in these last days, just prior to Christ's coming?' That's a magnificent question! Let us read what follows after these three angel's messages:

> Then I heard a voice from heaven saying to me, "Write: 'Blessed are the dead who die in the Lord from now on.'" "Yes," says the Spirit, "that they may rest from their labors, and their works follow them." Then I looked, and

behold, a white cloud, and on the cloud sat *One* like the Son of Man, having on His head a golden crown, and in His hand a sharp sickle. And another angel came out of the temple, crying with a loud voice to Him who sat on the cloud, "Thrust in Your sickle and reap, for the time has come for You to reap, for the harvest of the earth is ripe." So He who sat on the cloud thrust in His sickle on the earth, and the earth was reaped. Then another angel came out of the temple which is in heaven, he also having a sharp sickle. And another angel came out from the altar, who had power over fire, and he cried with a loud cry to him who had the sharp sickle, saying, "Thrust in your sharp sickle and gather the clusters of the vine of the earth, for her grapes are fully ripe." So the angel thrust his sickle into the earth and gathered the vine of the earth, and threw *it* into the great winepress of the wrath of God. And the winepress was trampled outside the city, and blood came out of the winepress, up to the horses' bridles, for one thousand six hundred furlongs. (Rev. 14:13–20)

Did you notice that right after the three angels' messages are preached "unto them that dwell on the earth, and to every nation, and kindred, and tongue, and people" (verse 6), the next thing that takes place is "the harvest of the earth"? Read again how John portrayed the harvest: "And another angel came out of the temple, crying with a loud voice to Him who sat on the cloud, 'Thrust in Your sickle and reap, for the time has come for You to reap, for the harvest of the earth is ripe'" (verse 15; a sickle was an instrument used in biblical times to harvest the crops of a farmer).

In the parable of the wheat and the tares, Jesus explained to His disciples, "The harvest is the end of the world; and the reapers are the angels. The Son of man shall send forth his angels, and they shall gather out of his kingdom all things that offend, and them which do iniquity; And shall cast them into a furnace of fire: there shall be wailing and gnashing of teeth" (Matt. 13:39–42, KJV).

At this point, I will share some fundamental answers to certain questions: Why is it taking so long for Jesus to return? Why is there such a long delay? As we probe deeper into these questions, we will discover more clues about these previously mentioned evil forces, sometimes referred to in the Bible as "Babylon," "beasts," "horns," "the son of perdition," or "the man of sin."

CHAPTER 19

NO NEED TO FEAR

"For God hath not given us the spirit of fear; but of power, and of love, and of a sound mind" (2 Tim. 1:7). When the Lord is our God, we have nothing to fear. He gives us His love, power, and a sound mind. Praise the Lord! Nevertheless, there are many scary passages in Scripture for the ones who have rejected God as their Lord and Savior. They have plenty of which to be afraid, especially those who are deceived in believing they are following God, only to discover, when it is too late, that they were not following Him at all.

This is how the Bible characterizes this dreadful deception:

> Not everyone who says to Me, "Lord, Lord," shall enter the kingdom of heaven, but he who does the will of My Father in heaven. Many will say to Me in that day, "Lord, Lord, have we not prophesied in Your name, cast out demons in Your name, and done many wonders in Your name?" And then I will declare to them, "I never knew you; depart from Me, you who practice lawlessness!" (Matt. 7:21–23, NKJV)

Frankly, I cannot think of a more devastating, disappointing situation. Imagine that for all your life, you were sure you were following Jesus, but at the end, you hear these solemn words straight from His mouth. The immediate question would be, "How might such a tragedy occur?"

The next passage is also dreadful passage to consider: "So the great dragon was cast out, that serpent of old, called the Devil and Satan, who deceives the whole world; he was cast to the earth, and his angels were cast out with him" (Rev. 12:9). This verse is referring to a great war that took place in heaven between the forces of God and the forces of Satan, who used to be named Lucifer.

Satan's rebellion had gotten so intolerable that he had to be cast out of heaven. Unfortunately, he eventually made his headquarters here on earth. I know what your next question might be: "Why did God not simply destroy the devil when he rebelled against his Maker in heaven?"

I used to be perplexed by that same question, and others, until I found the answers in the Bible. You see, the enemy was a wily foe. He was able to hide his deceptive plans from the rest of the hosts of heaven. Had God destroyed him right away, there would have been questions and uncertainties about God's character in the minds of the angels in heaven, and that could have led to an even more catastrophic rebellion. This was already bad enough! Earlier, I had discussed God's wonderful gift of the power of choice that can shed more light on this subject and others. For now, let me discuss a bit about the rebellion itself that started in heaven and is now raging on this planet.

My purpose here is simply to share with you some of my discoveries, of which you may be totally unaware. The Bible characterizes the mind and attitude of Lucifer this way:

> How you are fallen from heaven, O Lucifer, son of the morning! *How* you are cut down to the ground, You who weakened the nations! For you have said in your heart: "I will ascend into heaven, I will exalt my throne above the stars of God; I will also sit on the mount of the congregation on the farthest sides of the north; I will ascend above the heights of the clouds, I will be like the Most High." (Isa. 14:12–14)

Lucifer was not satisfied with being just a powerful created angel; he wanted to execute a coup to dethrone his Maker. He wanted the angels to worship him instead of worship God. Do not forget, dear reader, this issue is always about worship. We get a glimpse of the character of Satan when he tried to get the Son of God to worship him:

> Again, the devil took Him up on an exceedingly high mountain, and showed Him all the kingdoms of the world and their glory. And he said to Him, "All these things I will give You if You will fall down and worship me." Then Jesus said to him, "Away with you, Satan! For it is written, 'You shall worship the Lord your God, and Him only you shall serve.'" (Matt. 4:8–10)

Please notice Jesus did not get into a controversy with the enemy. He simply quoted Scripture. By the way, this is a very important lesson for those who encounter the devil—the wily foe. And that's another reason why we should study the Bible for ourselves: to know what God has to say. In fact, this is our only safeguard: to study the Bible and therefore learn to know the God of the Bible. Otherwise, the enemy will surely overcome us. We need the Holy Spirit to fill our minds with understanding of the Word of God.

Let us refer to Revelation 12:9 again: "So the great dragon was cast out, that serpent of old, called the Devil and Satan, who deceives the whole world; he was cast to the earth, and his angels were cast out with him." That was the same angel who was named Lucifer. He deceives people on earth, just as he did many angels in heaven, to get them to worship him instead of worship God.

One of the clever, subtle tactics of the devil is to use other people, especially powerful religious leaders, to do his deceptive work for him. Many people who sincerely believe they are worshipping the Living God are, in reality, following the devil and his false teachings. That is one of the reasons why many discerning people do not trust religious people who profess to be followers of God. Let us take another look back to Revelation 17 to make a connection. It is the impious harlot woman who persecutes God's people—the same who is "drunk with the blood of the saints and with the blood of the martyrs of Jesus."

Again, God's church is represented by a virtuous woman. A false church is described as a rebellious, unfaithful harlot. The following passage is just a sample: "I have likened the daughter of Zion to a lovely and delicate woman" (Jer. 6:2). This passage is definitely referring to a faithful church. The next passage sheds a little more light on understanding God's virtuous church:

> Now a great sign appeared in heaven: a woman clothed with the sun, with the moon under her feet, and on her head a garland of twelve stars. Then being with child, she cried out in labor and in pain to give birth. And another sign appeared in heaven: behold, a great, fiery red dragon having seven heads and ten horns, and seven diadems on his heads. His tail drew a third of the stars of heaven and threw them to the earth. And the dragon stood before the woman who was ready to give birth, to devour her Child as soon as it was born. She bore a male Child who was to rule all nations with a rod of iron. And her Child was caught up to God and His throne. (Rev. 12:1–5)

The above passage not only mentions a woman (God's church), but it calls attention to the dragon, identified as Satan (see verse 9), who stands in front of the woman who was about to give birth to a child "who was to rule all nations." This is undoubtedly referring to when Mary was giving birth to baby Jesus, who is the true Ruler of all nations. This passage also refers to the people of God from whom Jesus was born. The woman who is called "the mother of harlots" is a religious, rich, blasphemous church that has many children (i.e., other churches) following her blasphemous, abominable doctrines. The kings, rulers, and people of the world who do not know God are just drinking it all in.

Furthermore, do you also notice how the dragon was cast out from heaven to the earth with one third of the stars (angels)? As mentioned previously, the dragon (devil) uses horns (earthly powers) to do his dirty work for him (ref. to Dan. 7:23, 24). Again, these can be civil or religious powers, just as the devil used Herod initially to try to kill baby Jesus. Then Pilate and the religious leaders were used to crucify Jesus. Dear reader, please don't ever forget that Satan always uses civil and religious powers to persecute God's true church/people. And as we get closer to the second coming of Christ, this type of persecution will intensify. "Yes, and all who desire to live godly in Christ Jesus will suffer persecution" (2 Tim. 3:12).

The following Bible verses are messages of encouragement when we are persecuted for serving Christ and the gospel:

- **Romans 8:35**: "Who shall separate us from the love of Christ? Shall tribulation, or distress, or persecution, or famine, or nakedness, or peril, or sword?"

- **Romans 12:14**: "Bless those who persecute you; bless and do not curse."

- **Matthew 5:10-12**: "Blessed *are* those who are persecuted for righteousness' sake, for theirs is the kingdom of heaven. Blessed are you when they revile and persecute you, and say all kinds of evil against you falsely for My sake. Rejoice and be exceedingly glad, for great *is* your reward in heaven, for so they persecuted the prophets who were before you."

- **Psalm 23:4**: "Yea, though I walk through the valley of the shadow of death, I will fear no evil; For You *are* with me; Your rod and Your staff, they comfort me."

- **2 Corinthians 12:10**: "Therefore I take pleasure in infirmities, in reproaches, in needs, in persecutions, in distresses, for Christ's sake. For when I am weak, then I am strong."

Beloved, let us not be afraid. We are to remain faithful to Jesus until the end. He will never leave or forsake us. Jesus is able to protect His own—those who are trusting Him—even though we are encircled by legions of evil angels.

CHAPTER 20

GOD'S PROMISES DELAYED

God has often delayed His promises in order to either give us more instruction with respect to important lessons we need to learn or show us obstacles that are keeping us from being ready for His kingdom. In the New Testament, we have Jesus' well-known promise: "Let not your heart be troubled; you believe in God, believe also in Me. In My Father's house are many mansions; if it were not so, I would have told you. I go to prepare a place for you. And if I go and prepare a place for you, I will come again and receive you to Myself; that where I am, there you may be also" (John 14:1-3). His promise is to return again and take us to heaven with Him.

Recently, I was watching a funeral service on television. A speaker—I am sure with good intentions—prayed to Jesus, Mary, and another "saint" in interceding for the deceased. I could not help but think of Jesus' words to His disciples: "I am the way, the truth, and the life. No one comes to the Father except through Me" (verse 6).

These words have been quoted by millions of Christians for ages, yet there true significance has never occurred to most. There are at least two other passages in Scripture that categorically forbid Christians to pray for forgiveness of sin to anyone except Jesus. If a person commits an infraction against another human being, he or she is admonished to go to that person and ask for forgiveness, but nowhere in the Bible are we commanded to ask another human being, religious or otherwise, for absolution or pronouncement of the remission (forgiveness) of sins to the penitent.

> Nor is there salvation in any other, for there is no other name under heaven given among men by which we must be saved. (Acts 4:12)
>
> For *there is* one God and one Mediator between God and men, *the* Man Christ Jesus, who gave Himself a ransom for all, to be testified in due time. (1 Tim. 2:5, 6)

This means Jesus is the only Mediator/Intercessor between God and humanity. We do not need to pray to Saint Peter, Saint Mary, Saint Paul, or any other "saints." These people are asleep, waiting for the resurrection, just like the rest of the deceased are.

We need to understand the Greek-based term "antichrist" does not exclusively mean "against Christ." There is another subtle definition: "In place of Christ." The "man of sin" will not come out openly against Christ. "Who is a liar but he that denies that Jesus is the Christ? He is antichrist, that denies the Father and the Son" (1 John 2:22). The antichrist will put another "savior" or "saviors" in place of Christ. While we are waiting and looking for the antichrist to come, he is very prominent right before our eyes, hiding, as it were, in broad daylight. He even exhorts the name of Jesus when it is convenient while simultaneously exhorting himself as His vicar on earth.

We get another clue from Paul regarding the second coming of Christ being delayed. There are some prophesies that first need to be fulfilled:

> Let no one deceive you by any means; for *that Day will not come* unless the falling away comes first, and the man of sin is revealed, the son of perdition, who opposes and exalts himself above all that is called God or that is worshiped, so that he sits as God in the temple of God, showing himself that he is God. Do you not remember that when I was still with you I told you these things? And now you know what is restraining, that he may be revealed in his own time. For the mystery of lawlessness is already at work; only He who now restrains *will do so* until He is taken out of the way. And then the lawless one will be revealed, whom the Lord will consume with the breath of His mouth and destroy with the brightness of His coming. The coming of the *lawless one* is according to the working of Satan, with all power, signs, and lying wonders, and with all unrighteous deception among those who perish, because they did not receive the love of the truth, that they might be saved. (2 Thess. 2:3–10)

According to Paul, there are several things that need to happen before Jesus returns. A "falling away comes first." In other words, there will be a great apostasy in the church of God before the second coming. Next, "the man of sin," who is also called "the son of perdition" and "the lawless one" is to be revealed or unmasked. Third, this antichrist "sits as God in the temple of God, showing himself that he is God" (verse 4). He even takes prerogatives that belong only to God. No wonder Paul warns God's true believers to not be deceived "by any means" (verse 3). Let us examine a subtle deception against which we need to guard.

"Little children, it is the last hour; and as you have heard that the Antichrist is coming, even now many antichrists have come, by which we know that it is the last hour … And every spirit that does not confess that Jesus Christ has come in the flesh is not of God. And this is the *spirit* of the Antichrist, which you have heard was coming, and is now already in the world" (1 John 2:18; 4:3).

If one is interested in more accurately identifying who "the man of sin" or antichrist is, one has to start the search for a system whose origin is from a long time ago. Its development started even during the early days of the Christian church. Any person or system that offers any other intercessor besides Jesus Christ is the antichrist.

Yes, it is so simple! No matter how religious or pious a person may appear, the Word of God makes it perfectly clear. "[Jesus] is the propitiation for our sins, and not for ours only but also for the whole world" (2:2). Jesus paid the price for all our sins. Furthermore, "Yet for us *there is* one God, the Father, of whom *are* all things, and we for Him; and one Lord Jesus Christ, through whom *are* all things, and through whom we *live*" (1 Cor. 8:6).

Therefore, it is necessary for every sincere follower or seeker of God to pray *only* to Jesus for the forgiveness of one's sins. Do not allow any false prophets to deceive you by stating that another intercessor is needed to plead for you in heaven. Not only would that be an exercise in futility but also a great deception. Please do not forget, beloved, the antichrist is anyone who takes the place of or is in addition to Jesus

The biblical promises concerning the return of Christ also remind me of another reason why His return is delayed. Let me use an illustration. Imagine you were going to an airport to fly somewhere. One of the first things you do when entering an airport is find the departure board in order to check the flights scheduled on the monitors. You want to know the status of your flight. This is also true of the coming of Christ. His flight seems to be delayed. I am confident that even though the flight may seem to be delayed, it is not cancelled. Thank God, He keeps His promises. Perhaps this flight is delayed because the passengers are busy with the cares of this world, their hearts have become hard, or some may even be procrastinating.

Furthermore, one may liken the delay to a plane circling around an airport waiting for the problems or conditions on earth's tarmac to be resolved. What a flight that will be to go to heaven with Jesus! Again, thank God, the flight is just delayed; it is not cancelled. The worst problem is that some will still miss the flight due to their unbelief and rebellion. Many have become careless and lazy in the cause and work of God. However, as we get nearer to the end, the preparation needs to become more intense, not less. And since God is not willing that any should perish, He continues to reason with us, hoping we will allow Him to change our hearts before it is too late.

Even though the flight is delayed, we all can still make the flight. "For you have need of endurance, so that after you have done the will of God, you may receive the promise: 'For yet a little while, *And* He who is coming will come and will not tarry. Now the just shall live by faith; But if *anyone* draws back, My soul has no pleasure in him'" (Heb. 10:36–38). Our employment and other cares of this world sometimes feel like chains around our necks. We get entangled in the "system." We believe we have an obligation to "keep up with the Joneses."

The promise of Jesus' soon coming is often a distant-second priority in our minds, if we give it even a fleeting thought. The long, wearisome delay since that promise has caused many to relax their vigilance. We must not surrender to this deception or lose hope in the promise. We are to be busy during this final preparation. We need to be on our knees more often, as the following illustration points out:

Sir George Adam Smith (Scottish Bible scholar and Old Testament professor) told how he and his guide were climbing a mountain in the Swiss Alps. It was stormy, and they were making their climb on the sheltered side of the peak. When they reached the summit, they were filled with so much excitement. Sir George leaped up in celebration and was nearly blown over the edge to the glacier below by a gust of fierce wind. Fortunately, the guide quickly grabbed hold of him. As the guide held onto him, Sir George heard him exclaim, "On your knees, sir. You are safe here only on your knees."

This is not the time to lessen our vigilance! We are in the final days! We are to be on our knees. "Pray without ceasing" (1 Thess. 5:17). "But he who endures to the end shall be saved" (Matt. 24:13). Just because waiting for Christ's second coming seems to be taking a very long time, we have to see by faith that the promise will surely be fulfilled. This lesson of Jesus is also confirmed by John. With this information in mind, do you see why these messages in Revelation are so urgent? We need to be *ready* in order for Jesus to fulfill His promises completely when He returns for us. When we are ready, we will have no need to fear!

EPILOGUE

In these last days, we are to be like Moses, who renounced the luxurious life in Egypt to adopt God's way.

By faith Moses, when he became of age, refused to be called the son of Pharaoh's daughter, choosing rather to suffer affliction with the people of God than to enjoy the passing pleasures of sin, esteeming the reproach of Christ greater riches than the treasures in Egypt; for he looked to the reward. By faith he forsook Egypt, not fearing the wrath of the king; *for he endured as seeing Him who is invisible.* (Heb. 11:24–27, emphasis added).

Beloved, just because something is invisible does not mean it is without effect. I have testified how God has blessed and continues to bless me today. Think of magnetism, wind, radiation, and germs. None are visible to the naked eye, but their respective effects can be extraordinarily clear. Though God is invisible, His effect in our lives can be amazing as well, just as it was in the life of Moses. He had real faith in God; so must we! We are to be the ones who are "looking unto Jesus, the author and finisher of *our* faith, who for the joy that was set before Him endured the cross, despising the shame, and has sat down at the right hand of the throne of God" (12:2, NKJV).

Paul encouraged his readers with these words:

Not that I have already attained, or am already perfected; *but I press on*, that I may lay hold of that for which Christ Jesus has also laid hold of me. Brethren, I do not count myself to have apprehended; but one thing [I do,] forgetting those things which are behind and reaching forward to those things which are ahead, *I press toward the goal for the prize of the upward call of God in Christ Jesus.* Therefore let us, as many as are mature, have this mind; and if in anything you think otherwise, God will reveal even this to you. Nevertheless, to [the degree] that we have already attained, let us walk by the same rule, let us be of the same mind. (Phil. 3:12–16, emphasis added).

I do hope and pray these few explanations from this simple Bible student will help you understand a little more clearly what God's Word really teaches. Furthermore, it is my prayer that this book will lead you to investigate more deeply these truths before it is too late. May God richly bless you. Maranatha (our Lord is coming)!

TEACH Services, Inc.
P U B L I S H I N G

We invite you to view the complete
selection of titles we publish at:
www.TEACHServices.com

We encourage you to write us
with your thoughts about this,
or any other book we publish at:
info@TEACHServices.com

TEACH Services' titles may be purchased in
bulk quantities for educational, fund-raising,
business, or promotional use.
bulksales@TEACHServices.com

Finally, if you are interested in seeing
your own book in print, please contact us at:
publishing@TEACHServices.com

We are happy to review your manuscript at no charge.

www.ingramcontent.com/pod-product-compliance
Lightning Source LLC
Chambersburg PA
CBHW070543170426
43200CB00011B/2530